MW01643848

The Will to Laugh

On the Brink of Irrational Optimism

Jeffrey and Devon Smith

Illustrated by Elliana Englund

Scripture versions used:

THE WILL TO LAUGH

First Printing, 2022.

ISBN 979-8-218-08053-2

Printed in the United States of America.

Dedication

In honor of my mom, who taught me how to fight and scarcely feel the bruises.

Table of Contents

Acknowledgements

To my wife Devon—without her wit, funny perspective on life and most of all, unflagging devotion and faith in her husband, this book would never have come to be. She has given me the best 18 years of my life.

To my talented illustrator and graphic designer Elliana, who patiently listened to my babbling as I formed ideas. She adroitly captured and improved on the images in my mind. Her creative suggestions and hard work exceeded my expectations.

To my editor and sister-in-law Mollie, whose attention to detail, contributions that enhanced the clarity of my ideas and her overall cheerful nature has been invaluable. How difficult it would have been to create a quality book without her skills.

To my mom, who had the same expectations of me as her other children to overcome obstacles despite my challenges. Her forward thinking propelled me to become the man I am today.

And to my buddies Mark R., Don, Scott, Craig, Tom, Kathy, and Mark M., who have encouraged me, supported me, and helped me build my "empire," or so they let me believe. They have smoothed my rough edges, entertained me and been a delight. I can never repay them.

Introduction

The impetus for this book was an event that would change our lives and how we were to view our future. For 23 years, I had been America's only blind magician. At least as far as I could see! For 25 years, Devon had worked with adults and children in Community Education.

One day in Spring of 2016, our lives were turned upside-down. Devon was returning home from a transitional, part-time job, which would be a bridge to joining me with my magic and motivational speaking business. While waiting for a freeway gridlock to loosen, she was rear-ended at 60 miles per hour.

After most of her physical injuries had begun to heal, Devon was diagnosed with Post-Concussive Syndrome (PCS). This left her with visual impairments preventing her from driving, and other effects of a traumatic brain injury (TBI), which deplete the majority of her cognitive and physical energy on a daily basis.

After more than three years of treatment and therapies, we learned her deficits were most likely permanent and would rule out our plan for her to market, drive me, and assist at presentations. In one pivotal moment, she also lost her ability to easily pursue her passions for reading, creative writing, and travel. Even simple activities take a toll on her energy and cognitive ability.

With the pathway to our future plans suddenly barricaded, requiring major lifestyle changes, our initial response was filled with anxiety and trepidation.

But since we had professed throughout our marriage of thirteen years to be Christians, and trusted God's promise to provide in all situations, now was the time to lean on Him and test His assurances.

Being home-based for the most part, how could we productively use our newfound time? Given that we are two people who enjoy expressing ourselves, naturally favorable circumstances arose to muse, reflect, and observe life around us. (It's also true that this concentrated living together concept included many instances of driving each other up the wall. But oh, the laughs we harvested later!)

Over the course of time, what we knew to be true was reinforced: that our commonalities with each other outweigh our differences. We are imperfectly normal, or, call it "normally imperfect"...because isn't human imperfection really the norm? And, may I add, *in the most delightful manner!?* After all, isn't that what makes living and interacting interesting, funny, intriguing, fascinating, and exciting!

This book has real-life examples of humor within our marriage and life, that uplift us amidst the challenges we encounter, interspersed with some of our favorite jokes that continually tickle us. It is our sincere hope that the humor on these pages will encourage, amuse, and entertain you as you manage your own daily trials, come what may!

♦ Chapter 1 ♦

Altogether Devon

"A woman with visual challenges, but with a clear vision of fun."
—Jeff Smith

I learned years ago, or at least several weeks ago, you can catch more flies with honey than vinegar. That is why the first thing I said to Devon after returning from an errand was, "Thank you so much for packing and addressing envelopes to ship my new book orders."

Devon replied, "Actually, I haven't done that yet."

Trying to still show general appreciation, I responded, "Well, thank you for your willingness to pack and address my books."

Devon answered, "I'm actually doing it against my will."

"Oookaaayyy, let me rephrase it for the third time..."

Flexibility is not just a term reserved for acrobats.

✧ ✧ ✧

Upon publication of my second book, Devon noticed her name, for the first time, as the co-author.

"You have my name on the cover?!"

I replied, "Of course! You really contributed, not only proofing things, but by being the unwitting supplier of so many wisecracks."

Devon paused and slowly left the room as I heard her mumble, "I'm an author...I'm an author." Yet still near enough to hear me say, "Your name will heretofore be rightfully displayed on every future book."

Now she insists on final approval of anything about her and anything in general.

I am slumming with a product of Mary Shelley's imagination!

Around the house, I'm always humming tunes that are most often unrecognizable to others. I've been called a "jailhouse" singer—behind a few bars, and I can't find the key!

Recently, I approached Devon and said, "Listen Honey, don't you think this tune I made up sounds like something in the vein of Duke Ellington?"

After patiently hearing my new creation, she said, "You sure have a lot of bending notes in your song."

I replied, "Those aren't bending notes; they're minor notes, honey."

Devon responded, "MINOR is definitely right!"

Devon sighed, "I don't so much mind being middle-aged, except when I feel like that's when I was born."

During a serious dialogue between Devon and me regarding a deep, complex Biblical truth, Alexa evidently felt she needed to contribute and interjected, "Asian food is food from Asia."

Devon sighed and said, "Ahhh...! Thank you, Alexa, for clearing up that mystery."

With confidence swelling, Alexa responded, "You're welcome. Have a nice day."

At some point, we are hoping Devon will be able to drive again. I am certainly not going to stand in her way.

Today I noticed Devon had a little extra spirit in her step, a little more crispness in her voice, enough to ask her, "So what's up with you?"

"Well, since you asked, as your legally authorized Personal Support Staff, I just received an e-mail from the county declaring me as a 'critical worker', just in case you weren't aware of it."

"Well, I've certainly been aware of at least a good half of that for a long time!"

I asked my significant other, "Did you know there are no canaries in the Canary Islands? The same is true of the Virgin Islands...There are no canaries there either."

I cannot tell you how many times I must remind Devon: "It's my personality, charm, and wit that keeps you attracted."

"Truth be told," Devon mused, "don't underestimate your role as my scullery boy."

Trying to be humble, I responded, "Well, any help I can give you around the house, I enjoy doing. What do you particularly appreciate about my role as your scullery boy?"

Quickly Devon answered, "I love seeing you over a hot sink of dishes—shirtless, wearing nothing but a fine sheen of sweat."

Sensing my sudden nervousness, she added, "It sort of gives me a little taste of the power of Cleopatra."

When Devon saw her first strands of grey hair, she thought she would dye!

✧ ✧ ✧

From the next room, Devon exclaimed, "They're coming out with a live action version of *Dumbo*!"

Being one of the most tender-hearted people I know, I heard Devon quietly begin singing the theme song from the Disney classic.

Next, I heard her say, "I think I'm going to cry."

Feeling snarky, I suggested, "How 'bout we watch *Bambi* instead."

Lacey, Devon, and I were watching a really corny 1950's movie, meant to be serious, called *Hell and High Water*. I was taking lots of liberty, making snide remarks and wisecracks, with all the opportunities the movie presented.

"Now stop that! Just stop!"

Confused, I said, "Are you talking to me?"

"No. Lacey is bugging me. But you're next!"

✧ ✧ ✧

Devon shared an interesting fact with me about bees. When she finished, I remarked, "You know, it's funny you telling me that story about bees, because just today I had a long conversation about bees."

Giggling, Devon asks, "With yourself?"

I just replaced our bed with a trampoline. Oh boy, did Devon hit the roof!

"As long as you're up, can you get me something to munch on?"

"I just read something in the Bible, which reminds me of our relationship."

Devon asked, "And what would that be?"

"When I finally become sleepy, the ceasing of chatter reminds me of what Jesus said to his disciples at the Last Supper. He said, '...you will grieve, but your grief will turn to joy. A woman giving birth to a child has pain...but when her baby is born she forgets the anguish because of her joy...'"[1]

Devon replied, "So where exactly is the tie-in with me?"

I answered, "That verse is meant for you! Before I fall asleep is like you giving birth...and after comes the joy!"

We had one of those Kirby vacuum salesmen give us a demonstration. Afterward, he said, "Lady, this vacuum cleaner will cut your work in half."

Devon quickly responded, "Good. I'll take two of them."

✧ ✧ ✧

As I talked to my mom on the phone, Devon entered the room following her shower. Hoping Devon would overhear, I said to Mom, "Oh. It smells like Devon has entered the room."

Mom responded, "Oh, really?"

"Yes. She smells like a garden in full bloom."

Devon added, "I should smell like I'm in bloom. Before my shower, I smelled like fertilizer!"

From the living room, Devon shrieked, "It's April 10th and the forecast is for snow!"

To calm her alarm, I said, "Just think of the soft white fluffy flakes as little bunnies from heaven."

Devon responded, "More like little bunny *droppings* from heaven."

Devon said to a dear friend of ours, "I understand you and my husband are going bar hopping."

"We're too old for hopping! Once we arrive, that's where we stay. You can call it bar flopping."

✧ ✧ ✧

One Sunday, Devon decided she'd like to try out the church I attend. I'm typically picked up by a family of six, not counting me.

"I hope they have enough room for me, Jeff."

"Relax, I have it all figured out. We'll all wear red rubber noses, and right after church, we're going to unload at the circus!"

✧ ✧ ✧

We thought we were watching an autobiography of Helen Keller, imaginatively depicted from her own point of view. It took everything we had to stay interested in the movie.

Then we realized the picture tube had gone out a while ago.

After finishing a movie on her iPad, Devon looked up and noticed I was engrossed in a movie about one of the iconic Pacific Ocean battles in the war against Japan.

She commented, "You're obviously not ready for bed. I see you're in the middle of a World War II flick."

I responded, "To be accurate, 'midway' would be the more proper term."

At Devon's request, I took a course in modesty. I am proud to say I finished head of the class!

Having reached her conversation threshold for the day, Devon suggested, "Hey! Let's watch a movie."

We started watching the remake of the movie, *The Fly*, starring Jeff Goldblum.

I said, "Isn't Goldblum also the guy on *Jurassic Park*? What part did he play?"

Devon offhandedly responded, "He plays the nerd who talks and talks and talks."

I responded, "Wait! What was that?"

Quickly correcting herself, Devon said, "Err...uhh...I mean the cool guy who talks and talks and talks."

Satisfied, I quipped, "I love that guy."

I was waxing rhetorically as I speculated on developing a new TV series.

"How about a series called *Dr. Pimple Popper Gets Squeezed.*"

Expanding my stream of consciousness, I continued to elaborate, "The show would be based on episodes of *Dr. Pimple Popper* that never aired, perhaps because of a medical mishap?"

This inspiration came immediately after viewing an episode called "Correcting a Gluteal Cleft."

Notching up my excitement, I added, "With all due sympathy toward the misfortunate patient, who wouldn't want to see a lost episode of someone's backside bouncing along behind them?"

Devon sighed and said, "You spend way too much time in your head."

✧ ✧ ✧

I overheard Devon telling a friend, "I haven't talked to Jeff for 18 months; I don't want to interrupt him."

✧ ✧ ✧

Lately, so many people come and go from our house, that Devon is overwhelmed.

To quiet things down, she suggested, "When we have someone over, let's serve them a bowl of peanuts. After they've eaten a few handfuls, we can casually mention we've never liked peanuts ourselves, but we sure love to suck the chocolate off them!"

"Who says a little saliva can't aid in digestion?"

Devon cherishes her time with *Judge Judy* every afternoon. Rewarding herself after completing tons of paperwork one day, Devon flipped on the show. But immediately she heard only a computer voice telling her about impending bad weather, rather than what she really longed for, Judge Judy's verbal fury, sarcastic inflections and insults—exactly the parts she loves the most. Frustrated, after many minutes hearing only the droning computer voice, she wailed, "I've got nothing against the safety of Beltrami, Minnesota, wherever that is, but why do they keep going on and on?"

Being confused as well, I casually commented that the computer voice sounded a little peppy for a weather alert, and strangely familiar to me. "Wait a minute," I said, "I think that's the same voice I hear when I turn on the feature that allows a blind person to navigate the TV menu."

Devon toggled that button and instantly the computer voice ceased and we became bathed in the unforgiving tones of Judge Judy as she howled at her litigants.

"If you hadn't said that Jeff, I don't know how long I'd be hearing the computer voice reading the emergency alert on the screen."

"Well, it does take two heads to run a village."

Devon suggested, "Maybe we can go for a walk tomorrow."

I responded, "No. The weather forecast said it's not going to be nice until Sunday."

Devon quipped, "What a coincidence! I don't plan on being nice until Sunday either."

✧ ✧ ✧

The other night, Devon said, "Now, after I serve you strawberries and whipped cream, I want it quiet around here. I'm going to be out for the count. No conversations and no questions."

Innocently I responded, "What possibly could I say about anything?"

Devon retorted, "The question every morning upon waking is 'Lord, what will he say today about EVERYTHING?'"

Devon told me to stop impersonating a flamingo.

I had to put my foot down.

Talking with food in my mouth is a real pet peeve for Devon.

Last night, during dinner, Devon noticed some tape stuck to my sock, which, unbeknownst to me, she discreetly removed as I was vigorously chewing a piece of meat, being sure to keep my mouth closed.

Before I could even swallow my bite, Devon added, "Well, you could have at least said 'thanks'."

I just mentally shrugged.

✧ ✧ ✧

At the mall, instead of taking the escalator like me, Devon took the stairs.

We were obviously raised differently.

After gently chiding a magic show driver/assistant for not remembering an item we typically take, Devon quickly scolded me, "Don't berate Debbie."

Feeling convicted, I tried covering my tracks, "I didn't *B-rate* her. I *A*-rate her!"

Devon retorted, "Just so you don't *I*-rate her."

✧ ✧ ✧

Devon never claimed to be a student of major league baseball.

"I didn't realize the Twins were in this year's World Series," she said after glancing up at the broadcast.

"No, the Twins actually are not in this year's Series, but what made you think that?" I asked.

"Well, I think I recognize the shape of home plate from watching them at Target Field."

✧ ✧ ✧

As Devon went to serve the pie which had only three pieces left, I announced, "I'll take two pieces, please."

Annoyed, she spouted, "That's not fair!"

"Yes, it is. The democratic system is 'two-thirds majority rules!'"

Trying to be helpful, I suggested I would carry my 30-ounce glass of morning beverage over to the table. Concerned, Devon asked, "Can you safely carry it without spilling?"

"Don't worry. If I start to fall, I'll just quickly drink it."

"Like I told you before, it's all under control!"

Shortly after awakening this morning, I said to Devon, "I had a strange and vivid dream. In the dream, I enter the monastery, and I must take a vow of silence, but once a year, I can write minimally on the chalkboard in front of the head monk.

"So, the first year goes by, it has been tough not to talk, but Word Day rolls around, and I write on the chalkboard: FOOD STINKS.

"The second year of silence is exceedingly difficult not to talk, but Word Day rolls around, and I write on the chalkboard: BED HARD.

"Excruciatingly, I finish my third year, and finally, Word Day rolls around. I write on the chalkboard: SORE KNEES.

"The head monk says, 'What's with you? You've been here for three years, and all you've done is complain!'"

Patiently waiting for me to finish my worn-out joke, Devon responded, "You taking a vow of silence?! That was definitely a dream. You don't even stop talking in your sleep!"

Devon, who lately is experiencing insomnia as a result of her second concussion, asked me in a tired voice this morning, "What does it mean when you have dark circles under your eyes that go down to your chin?"

"Don't be so hard on yourself. It's probably just mascara from your tears, worrying if you *have* dark circles under your eyes."

We were listening to a podcast of R.C. Sproul, who is a Bible teacher. To make a larger point he was using the account of David vs. Goliath. Being the class clown that I am, whether in the formal classroom or hanging out at home, I interrupted Mr. Sproul's story with what I imagined to be Goliath's taunt to the Israelites, "*Na-na-nana-na-na!!*"

Sproul then said something like: "Goliath said to the Israelites, 'Give me your best warrior, and I will fight him *mano a mano!*'"

Contributing her part to the irreverence, Devon interjected, "I didn't know Goliath spoke Spanish!"

Because I'm always a step behind Devon's quick wit, I asked her, "*Na-na-nana-na-na* is Spanish??"

Devon is so dang competitive. Lately we've both been walking on the treadmill. The other day I reached .44 of a mile. Yesterday, she matched that figure. Today, I could not seem to convince her that my going .45 of a mile was coincidental.

Before surgery, the removal of jewelry is required. After I had a couple of surgeries within a short period, Devon came to the realization that something was missing from my finger. Annoyed, she asked, "Why haven't you ever put your wedding ring back on?"

Defending myself, I replied, "Because it cuts off my circulation."

She quickly responded, "I know. It's supposed to."

Arriving early to my doctor appointment, Devon said, "Let me read you some news from my phone."

After a considerable delay I asked, "Is there something wrong?"

"I can't seem to close this silly ad!" exclaimed my frustrated wife.

As understanding suddenly dawned on her, she sheepishly added, "I can't close the ad because the 'ad' is a business card from our driver covering my screen perfectly."

✧ ✧ ✧

Devon read a tweet about a husband who was down with a cold and could not do anything himself. Devon mused, "You, on the other hand, aren't a baby when you're sick."

She giggled and added, "You don't need to be. You get the same things on a daily-basis anyway: 'Could you pull the blanket over my feet? Will you rub my head? How 'bout some coffee?'"

How sad! There is no advantage whatsoever to me getting sick.

✧ ✧ ✧

I do not understand how Devon could not have anticipated this happening. She fractured one of her little phalanx bones in her foot while hiking on, where else?

Krakatoa.

✧ ✧ ✧

It's been raining for three days without stopping. Devon has been so depressed. She just stands there looking through the window.

If the rain doesn't stop tomorrow, I'll have to let her in.

March is Women's Month and Brain Injury Awareness Month. I shiver when I ponder that the deficits of the latter could cause Devon to forget her awareness of being the former.

I had some particularly important, random thoughts to share with Devon, but apparently, she felt otherwise: "I told you before, I'm trying to read this e-book. I'm becoming annoyed!"

"Okay. I'll quit disturbing you."

"That's what you say," sighed Devon.

"...and I'll keep saying it over and over, all day if I have to, just to convince you."

Already in the midst of a frustrating day, Devon said to me, "Between your corny jokes and your lousy bathroom aim, you need a lot of work on your rim shots!"

✧ ✧ ✧

Surprisingly, one of the things I like best about Devon is her sarcasm.

As she described some e-mailed pictures of my performance in the park, I went off on a bit of a tangent.

After collecting my thoughts, I asked, "So the little volunteer is looking at me?"

"Yes. She still is."

After several arduous minutes painstakingly picking up my cane with my legs, I announced to Devon who was resting on the couch, "Honey! I saved you having to hop up by picking up my own cane!"

"I really appreciate your tremendous effort."

"Any time, baby!"

She added, "Except next time, right?"

In the most pathetic voice, I added, "Yeah, 'cause it was really, really hard!"

I am envious of Devon learning Korean, so I have taken up German. Yesterday I asked her what she thought about a phrase I said in German.

She responded, "If you want to sound like a real German, you have to use more *ex-Prussian* in your voice!"

My long-haul trucker buddy and I were on the topic of the late Howard Hughes, the eccentric billionaire who had an obsession about hand washing.

"I wouldn't admit to having an obsession about that, but when I'm busily knocking germs off my hands, Devon calls me 'Little Otter'."

"Are you sure she's not saying that more than any person she's ever met, you're a 'little odder'?"

Expressing my frustration, I cried, "Darn it! I was just about to load a pouch into my magic trick trunk...and I dropped it on the floor! Sorry, but would you please pick it up?"

As Devon got off the couch, she responded, "I can empathize with your frustration."

Still frustrated, I said, "The difference is, when you drop something, you're able to pick it up."

"Well, I have to pick it up either way!"

Her comment triggered an idea! Recently, Devon gained a few pounds due to ratcheting down her workout program following her second concussion this summer, obviously frustrating her. To help control this frustration until she can resume her program, and so she can stay calm whenever I bug her to pick something up, I devised a solution:

"Whenever I need you to pick up something I drop, I can remind you that any lingering weight is justified because you're eating for two."

Confused, Devon asked, "Eating for two?!"

I explained, "You have to keep up your calories when you're picking up for both of us!"

How could I have made such a mistake?

I accidentally gave Jeff a glue stick instead of *ChapStick*. He still is not talking to me.

I really should change the labels back, first thing tomorrow.

♦ Chapter 2 ♦

A Bump in the Road & On the Head

"It's keeping level amidst the bumps." –Devon Smith

Thank God He has given Devon and me an appreciation of one another which every day we express by, one or the other, saying, "I love you."

This morning, Devon's coping abilities were being tested to their limits. She was trying to concentrate on complex insurance paperwork, our handyman was pounding and drilling, and I had a friend on speaker phone engaged in an animated conversation.

After the handyman left and I had finished my call, Devon realized she was overdue for a break.

After several minutes of silence, I cautiously said to Devon, "Can I tell you 'I love you' without getting my head bitten off?"

Quietly, yet laced in an ominous tone, Devon answered, "It might be safe in about 20 minutes."

I know people who will never have a concussion because a concussion presumes one has a brain. Thus is my attempt at mindless humor.

✧ ✧ ✧

Because of symptoms that can suddenly arise with having a traumatic brain injury (TBI), it is difficult to plan outings with others. Yesterday, after we had to unexpectedly cancel an outing, I commiserated with Devon, "There's just no other way to call this TBI thing than what it is—a social disease."

She responded, "You might have given that thought a little more time to develop, dear."

When I asked Alexa to play a particular podcast, she responded, "Sorry, I am having trouble understanding right now. Please try again later."

Overhearing our cylindrically shaped housemate, Devon, who deals daily with the effects of a TBI amidst a noisy and overly bright environment, exclaimed, "We are soul sisters!!!"

✧ ✧ ✧

Devon was explaining to me, in a simplified way, the physiology of her PCS (Post-Concussive Syndrome).

"It's like this," she began, "Brain cell #1, 'Have a nice day!'"

"Brain cell #2, 'Have a good one!'"

"Devon's mouth, '*Haven gice done!*'"

✧ ✧ ✧

While she assisted me getting dressed for a doctor's appointment, Devon exclaimed, "I just remembered where I stashed some brand new, perfectly clean whitey tighties for you. I save them for when we have doctor appointments."

"I already have plenty of underwear."

"But these are to save yourself from being publicly embarrassed because of the looks of your everyday supply!"

That prompted me to say, "If you get approval to drive again and invite me on your inaugural trip, I just might need to wear one of those perfectly clean undies to look good in the ER."

Devon replied, "If my driving scares you that much, it seems like a moot point whether or not you begin with clean, white unders!"

"Have you seen a gas station yet?!"

I have a magic show this week in Truman, Minnesota. So, I thought I would take the opportunity to measure Devon's level of recovery from her recent concussion and test her mental acuity.

I posed to her, "Can you tell me where my magic show is on Friday? It's a city that's named after President Truman."

Devon responded, "I gather it's in Truman, Minnesota?"

In a voice laced with mock impatience, I answered, "Wrong! It's in President, Minnesota!"

Seems the part of Devon's brain that controls the annoyance response checks out A-ok, but I'm not gonna push it.

"Honey, I'd appreciate if you could quiet down for a bit before I begin to lose my patience."

Hearing Devon's tone of voice I thought, "Oops. I think it's too late."

I immediately moved all official chatty operations into my home office to give her brain some quiet.

After three hours, my jaws needed loosening up. Over the Alexa intercom that plays in the living room where she was resting, I cautiously asked, "Have I been in here long enough for you to miss me?"

Not skipping a beat, Devon answered, "I was just about to put you on my To-Do list!"

Due to a temporary lull in insurance coverage, Devon had to go a day without her medication called Amantadine. It helps increase her focus and concentration due to the TBI.

As Devon prepared my breakfast, she interrupted my idle chatter and said, "Don't say anything to me right now. Without my Amantadine in me, I need to really concentrate to make sure I actually pour the milk over your cereal and the water into your glass."

I replied, "Can't you simply refer to your recipe for water?"

In a steely voice, she answered, "Nope! I'm going commando!"

Do not presume we do not get some entertainment out of Devon's TBI. Today Devon suggested, "Since lately it's been chilly, how 'bout I make us some nice homemade Nicken Choodle soup?"

"Thure sing!" I replied.

I should have closed the bathroom door before starting, or, at least right away sprayed the air freshener. Afterward, with concern, I hollered into the next room, "Is everything okay out there?"

Devon cried out, "Yes, but until the air freshener kicked in, those were the longest four seconds of my life!"

I responded, "Well, that at least helps you understand Einstein's theory of relativity. You should recognize a clear case of *physics* when you smell it!"

O^2

Noticing me doze more than watch a movie with her, Devon decided to lay down the law and announced, "It's time for bed. You've snapped through half the movie!"

Confused, I responded, "Snapped?"

As she headed toward the bedroom, she explained, "Well, I was going to say 'snored'. Then I was going to say 'napped'. So, I guess that's where I got 'snapped'. Don't misunderstand...I don't have a brain injury...I made up a new word. Sorry you can't understand my new language."

Devon forcefully pulled the blanket off me last night. It took me a while to recover!

We're watching an old movie from the 1930's when an actor says in a Brooklyn accent, "There's nothin' woise than a two-timin' woman!"

Man! Can I identify! I had just asked Devon, "What time is it, honey?"

She responded, "It's 1:46...uh, I mean 1:36, uh-um...It's Wednesday, okay?"

Living with a two-timin' woman can take a *little* getting used to.

✧ ✧ ✧

I love our new bathroom spray. It completely neutralizes offensive odors. It's aptly named "Call-To-Duty".

I wonder sometimes if *I* must have gotten a bump on the head somewhere along the road. As I pondered away, before realizing it, I asked Devon, "Is a teacher who wears an eyepatch the effect or cause of a missing pupil?"

"What?!"

...I thought it best to resume my pondering.

✧ ✧ ✧

Although Devon manages technology quite adequately, she does not like it. In bed, I heard her yell from the living room, "When you go to bed you only leave me with the video remote! I always have to look for the audio remote!"

"I promise, tomorrow we'll sync both remotes to the cable system," I reassured.

She retorted, "It would be nice if you first 'sync' of me!"

Devon and I enjoy sitting together even if we end up focused on different things. I tend to hog the TV with the excuse that she has no interest in watching sports, while she immerses herself in iPad pursuits. Last evening, I turned on the Minnesota Timberwolves basketball game. In spite of her focus being on social media, dribs and drabs of the broadcast wafted into her consciousness.

"I'm so annoyed with that announcer! Why does he keep mentioning, 'bowel movement'? That's so disgusting!"

Scrunching my face, I responded, "Honey! He's not saying, 'bowel movement'. He's saying, 'ball movement'!" I'm surprised she didn't react to all the dribbling going on!!

25

• Chapter 3 •

A Dash of Sass & Hold the Filter

"'When the cookie crumbles, reach for your mom, the toughest cookie." –Donald A. Dinger (friend)

When my mom called today, I mentioned to her I was folding laundry. She responded, "You're 'Mother's Little Helper', huh?"

Chuckling, I added, "Do you know what 'Mother's Little Helper' actually refers to?"

Unwilling to wait, I said, "It stands for speed."

"Speed?"

"Yes. You know—a stimulant."

"What do you mean, a stimulant?"

Impatiently I blurted, "You know—something that makes you keep going."

"Oh, a laxative!"

✧ ✧ ✧

Enjoying my weekly Gin Rummy game with mom, to add a little variety to the routine, I pulled out my harmonica. "How about a little Elvis?"

After playing the tune, I realized I couldn't come up with the title. "Help me mom. I know it's one of his romantic songs."

She sighed and said, "I'm sorry. I can't help."

"That's it!!!"

"What?"

"*I Can't Help Falling in Love!*"

✧ ✧ ✧

My mom is offended, more than anything else in this world, by those who release gas in church. Being one who has always enjoyed stirring the pot, I asked her, "If you ruled the world, what would you do about those tooters in church?" In the vein of the Queen of Hearts in *Alice in Wonderland*, she bellowed, "I'd destroy them all!!"

Yakking with Mom on the phone, I shared news of my day, "I have a lunch date with my old speech pathologist."

Mom said, "She really straightened out your stutter, didn't she?"

"Well, there was once a time when I had something to say, but didn't, because it was just too much effort. Nowadays, I tend to err on the other side. I say something when I admittedly have nothing to say."

My supportive mother countered, "Well, that's your opinion."

"No. That's the opinion of everyone else."

Typically, I visit my mom weekly at her assisted living residence. I'm not going to tell you the name of the facility, in order to protect the innocent. Recently one of the staff told me about a little old lady who walked up to an old man and said, "If you drop your pants, I bet I can tell your age."

So, the old man dropped his pants, and she says, "You're 83 years old."

Astounded, he responded, "You're right! How could you tell?"

She said, "You told me yesterday."

I was raised as an only child, which really annoys my siblings.

My mom is in her seventh year at assisted living because of Alzheimer's. Early in the process of her dementia, my sister sent her a Keurig coffee machine. Recently, Mom mentioned she wasn't using it anymore. With as much as she enjoys a good cup of coffee, I knew this was due to her loss of ability, so I never talked about it again in order to not embarrass her.

Chatting with Mother over the phone this morning, I heard slurping. I asked, "Oh, are you still down in the dining room, having a cup of coffee?"

She answered, "No, I'm in my apartment having coffee."

"Oh, you must have brought a cup upstairs with you."

"No...I made this cup in my apartment."

Not having much else to talk about, and knowing she was out of coffee pods, I pursued the mystery: "But you are out of those coffee pods you need for your machine."

Becoming annoyed, she said, "I have a regular coffee pot."

Being drawn deeper into confusion, I said, "But you don't have the ground coffee beans you need for a regular coffee pot!"

Mom exclaimed, "Jeffrey, I don't need beans! I have a Keurig machine!"

I changed the subject.

✧ ✧ ✧

While playing Gin at Mom's, I repeated an earlier comment, "What a shame, the couple to whom we showed our rental unit couldn't afford it after all."

Mom responded, "I know that already. What I didn't know was that you were trying to rent it out."

After a long, fruitless discussion with my mom regarding someone at her assisted living building who she thought stole her newspaper from outside her apartment door, I needed to change the subject.

I suggested, "Have a little sympathy for the person."

"Why should I show any sympathy for someone who steals?"

Teasing, I said, "Well, Devon stole my heart, and I don't hold it against her."

My mom inquired, "Devon stole your heart?"

"She must have!" I said. "She's always calling me a *heartless lunk.*"

✧ ✧ ✧

Over the phone, my mom and I were comparing our outstanding characteristics. After I mentioned some of mine, Devon chimed in, "Don't forget about *talkative*."

Defending myself, I said, "For years, I could hardly talk due to my stuttering, so I really got pent up. Nowadays, I'm sort of verbally blowing my nose. I'm getting it aaaaall out."

Devon added, "...and you're getting it aaaaall over everyone."

✧ ✧ ✧

Rightfully or not, I usually feel the need to give Mom some advice to help improve her outlook. At the risk of encroaching on how she thinks and runs her life, in a small way I'm attempting to repay her for her years of care.

Bemoaning the loss of her once active social life, I tried to remind her what's truly important. "But really, Mom, when it comes down to it, what's more important—having had good communication in a marriage or lots of partying?"

Mom quickly responded, "Money for sure!"

I thought, "Just go with it, my friend."

The activity director at my mom's assisted living facility bought a copy of my autobiography. Afterward, I mentioned I was soon to come out with my second publication.

Seeing the director was impressed, my mom interjected, "My son is a very famous author. But we like to keep it in the family."

A Freudian slip is when you say one thing, but you mean your mother.

Throughout our marriage, I have had to remind Devon the common approach used by the Smith brothers to exchange family information. For purposes of expedience, we dispense of gentle, carefully thought-out phrasing. The focus is on facts, not presentation.

While playing a weekly card game, Mom and I were lamenting about how the family no longer gathers for holidays. "Mom, you were the maternal glue that held the family together, but now that you're a little dried up..."

Before I could rephrase my bluntness, Mom, used to this edginess, matter-of-factly responded, "I appreciate hearing that, Jeffrey. You're absolutely right!"

✧ ✧ ✧

I asked Mom, "If you could have a conversation with someone, living or dead, who would it be?"

"Definitely, I'd choose the one who's living."

While playing another game of Gin Rummy, my mom commented, "I wish there was some candy around here."

"Mom, I know you have a bag of Jolly Ranchers above your sink."

She checked and said, "Oh, I'm tired of hard candies."

"Well, for a change, maybe Devon can order you some butterscotch-flavored Werthers."

Mom quickly chirped, "Oh, yes! I like hard candies."

"Well, I know you have some Jolly Ranchers above your sink."

"Oh, goodie!"

Take it from an old advertising man, it's all in the packaging.

I am convinced sarcasm will be the last brain function to go in my mom. I mentioned to her, "We're going to a Korean restaurant for Devon's birthday. It's called 'Dong Hae'."

After several minutes of clarifying the name of the restaurant to Mom, she said, "Well, if *you're* going there, they should call it, '*Ding*-Dong Hae'."

Sharing mock hurt feelings over the phone with Devon, she consoled me: "When you get home, I'll give you some aloe for that burn!"

I get it coming AND going!

After losing the first three hands of cards to Mom, using my adapted cards, the score was 97 to 0.

I complained, "This is like taking candy from a baby!"

My mom retorted, "Worse than that, it's pathetic!"

Reconsidering my words, I said, "It's like playing cards with someone blind who's not using Braille cards!"

In a serious tone, Mom asked, "Why *don't* you get some Braille cards? Might help your game!"

I said my very first word the moment I entered the world. I said, "Wow!" I really wanted to say, "Mom," but I was being held upside down at the time.

✧ ✧ ✧

Never assume assisted living is full of sweet old ladies. Following a rare victory over my mother during our latest game of Gin, I said, "You have my condolences."

She retorted, "You can have those condolences back. In fact, you can stick 'em!"

Sweet...Old...Lady? Well, two out of three ain't bad, I guess.

✧ ✧ ✧

"You know Mom, if you can live another 14 years, you'll be 100 years old and likely be a great, great-grandmother."

"I think I'll pass."

✧ ✧ ✧

I was telling Mom about my great magic show today and how well-behaved the first and second-graders were. I also shared with her that the teachers were *first rate*.

"First grade teachers?! What teacher can be in first grade?" she cried.

Louder I said, "Mom, I said first RATE teachers!"

"I can't understand what you're saying."

Practically yelling I spelled it out, "R-A-T-E!" I followed this with an accidental, almost inaudible burp.

In an offended voice she said, "What do you say, Jeffrey?!"

"How can you hear my quiet little burp but can't hear me yelling the word RATE?!"

"Because you enunciate your burps."

Everyone has their cable TV niches. In my mom's case, she relishes the *I.D. network* (Investigation and Discovery). Predictably it recounts murders, some never having been solved. Devon, who regularly observes the schedule for programs Mom likes, noticed that the *I.D. network* was honoring the warmth and wonder of the season with their theme, "Vanished at Christmas." Amused, I reported to Mother, "Your favorite channel is running a Christmas special to capture the beauty and spirit of burglary, kidnap, and general mayhem."

With concern in her voice, she asked, "But I'll still get murder, right?"

✧ ✧ ✧

Yesterday, while enjoying a rare lead playing cards with Mom, she again stated, "I could hear you more clearly if you didn't mumble so much."

To further build the drama of the game, I said, "I know your strategy—until you're ready to go for the big kill, you're just giving me a false sense of confidence."

She responded, "A false sense of continence?! Not on my couch!"

"Oh...life would be so much easier if they only made hearing aids look like high fashion earrings."

As Mother's Alzheimer's progresses, she still maintains the ability to play Gin Rummy. Truth be told, she regularly kicks my butt. She can also be unintentionally funny. However, the style of humor is changing. While evaluating our card hands out loud I heard a huge belch immediately to my left. I knew it was not from me! I was startled, being used to my mom's elegant manners over the years that typically included hearing the most profuse apologies following the slightest faux pas, along the lines of, "I am so sorry! Please forgive me! I don't know where that came from!?"

Instead, I heard, "Hello!?"

Later, when I relayed this to Devon, she asked, "Did you laugh out loud?"

"No...I was busy recovering from my shock."

✧ ✧ ✧

Mom and I agreed that it was hard to imagine how anyone could go without breakfast before work. I tried to temper our feelings by adding, "I do have a friend who gets up at 4 a.m. for work. But he'll grab something to eat later at a break."

"What's his job?"

"He's a UPS driver. And according to the law, he must get breaks."

Mom said, "Of course he should get brakes; that's only common safety sense. Otherwise, just imagine the lawsuits!"

✧ ✧ ✧

After my mom received an order of tasty treats from us, she protested, "You don't expect me to eat these things. I'm going to get fat!"

"Mom. You can't get fat from unprocessed food like the kind we sent you: cashews, kalamata olives, mandarin oranges and the like. It's processed food that is the bad stuff."

She quipped, "You mean something like cherries from a chocolate-covered cherry tree?"

I reminded Mom that stuttering was a major challenge in my earlier years. Surprised, she inquired, "You were once a stutterer? You sure can't tell now!"

I responded, "The only time I ever stutter now is when I'm lying, which makes me not a very successful liar, at least according to Devon."

"So, you're saying, Jeffrey, you never stutter anymore?"

"N-n-n-o."

"Well, Jeffrey, I must admit, I am impressed!"

Making my weekly visit to Mother, we enjoyed our routine "sparring match" during our regular game of Gin.

Though my high-class mom and I often disagree, I think legendary singer Hank Williams correctly sized things up when he said: "There ain't no one in this here world that I'd rather have standin' next to me in a beer joint brawl than my Ma with a broken bottle in her hand."[2]

♦ Chapter 4 ♦

Eat, Drink & Be Married

I must be dyslexic. I eat ice cream, cake, chocolate, and sweets because "Stressed spelled Backwards is Desserts".
—Loretta LaRoche[3]

My enjoyment of the coffee drinking experience is based on many things, the least of which is its taste. I like the spark from its caffeine; I like the soothing quality of its warmth; I like the sensory impact from its brewing aroma. Devon even adds protein powder to it, at my request. As I luxuriously sipped this morning, I commented, "I'm really impressed how you so perfectly blend the protein powder into the coffee."

Devon responded, "Well, the powder is designed to be soluble, plus the heat from the coffee helps dissolve it." She paused a moment and added, "Forgetting today to add it to your coffee is also a factor to consider."

Practice safe eating—always use a condiment.

Growing up, my mom served lots of protein rich meals. Beef, beef, and more beef was her method to build sturdy framed kids. Every steer in the state gave her a wide berth. But now, being ever more aware of good heart health and the importance of being environmentally conscious, Devon and I have been motivated to make changes. We have, however, found the transition to be a bit difficult. We now rigorously prescribe to a weekly meal schedule that includes: Meatless Mondays, T-bone Tuesdays, Well-done Wednesdays, Thick-Cut Thursdays, Filet Fridays, Sirloin Saturdays, and Strip Sundays. After all, you can't just stop cold turkey...Cold turkey?

Mmm!

✧ ✧ ✧

Mixed Martial Arts has nothing over Mixed Nuts Arts, whose reigning champion is Cashew Clay.

✧ ✧ ✧

After coffee, I said to Devon, "Now I have an upset stomach."

"Well, why did you ask for coffee?"

"I didn't want to fall asleep in church."

"You could have tried Pepsi."

"Oh yeah, and then start burping in the middle of the sermon? 'Don't mind me, pastor, please continue...Braap.' Or, perhaps after a belch I could look to the side and just say in a disgusted voice, 'Laura! Excuse yourself!'"

Devon said, "Mature people would simply say excuse me."

"Could I at least say excuse me in a falsetto?"

She sighed, "How 'bout not saying anything at all?"

As an incredulous Devon cleared my plate, she declared, "You are such a messy eater! The only part of your fork that's clean are the tines."

✧ ✧ ✧

We have our groceries delivered. Recently one of the people who delivers shared with us her difficulty shopping.

"They only had one cart left, and it made a lot of noise, but I finally got it to work."

Devon empathized, "I totally understand. I have a husband just like that."

On the way home from a magic show my driver passed a roadside stand with a sign that read: "DONUTS 6-PACK".

I commented, "Wouldn't donuts and a 6-pack be an oxymoron?"

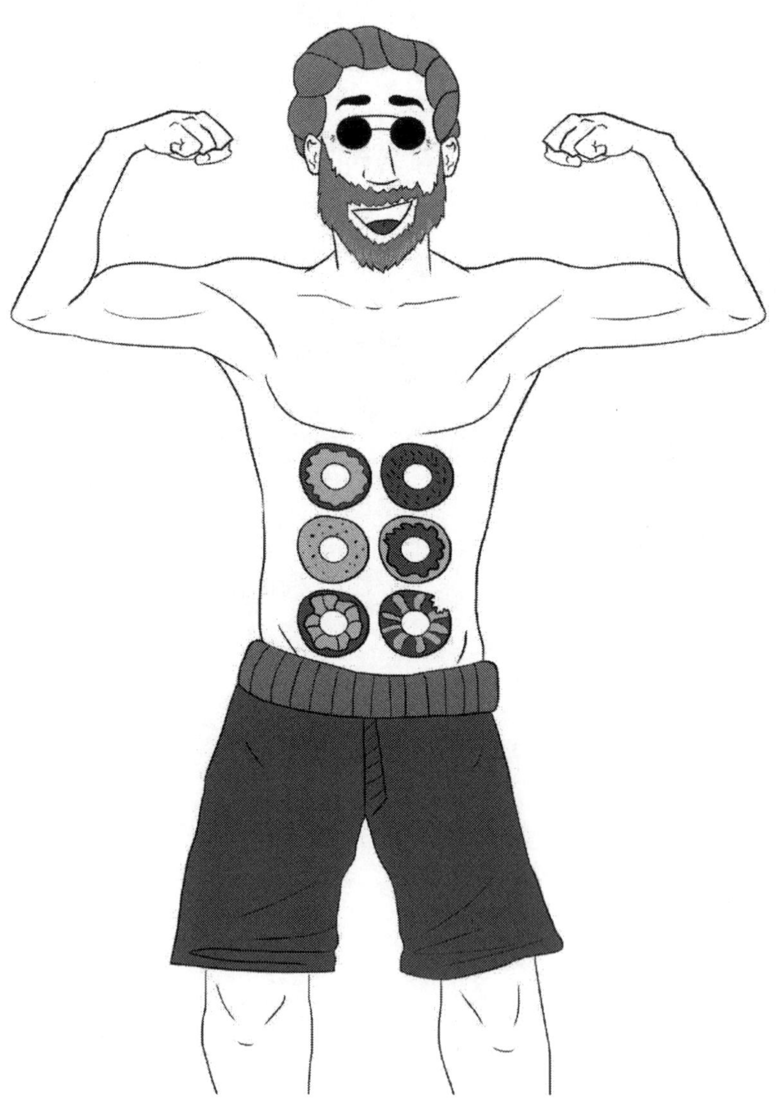

Did you hear about the kitchen designer arrested for counterfitting?

"Go out with a friend," Devon encouraged. "Don't let how I'm feeling keep you from getting your social fix that I know you need."

After I mentioned where my friend and I planned to go, Devon looked up their menu online and said, "Tonight they're having a deal on tacos. I know you like cheap."

Once we arrived, I told my buddy, "Well, I know what I'm having; it's Taco Tuesday."

He responded, "Isn't it Wednesday?"

"Dang it. Her bump on the head got me this time!"

Since I had my heart set on cheap tacos, I asked the server, "Can you ask the kitchen if they can make an exception and give me the same deal today?"

Returning, the server said, "I'm sorry. They can't make any exceptions."

At home, I shared the episode with Devon, "Hey, guess what? It's not Taco Tuesday."

Matter-of-factly, Devon said, "Maybe because the menu said taco day is Wednesday."

Frustrated that I didn't get my cheap tacos, I lamented, "You function better with a concussion than the restaurant staff who don't have bumps on their heads. About now, I think I could use a bump!"

What happens when you eat way too much alphabet soup?

You have a massive vowel movement.

We use a restaurant meal delivery service whenever Devon is having a bad brain injury day. They e-mailed us a $5 off coupon. Because Devon was having one of those days, I said, "Let's use that coupon tonight."

When she opened the email, she read that the coupon only applies to pickups.

Wow!

Just imagine...All we must do to have the privilege of using this company's generosity and be able to redeem our $5 coupon (a company who already limits your choices from the normal restaurant menu, plus adds a service charge to the regular price) is to *pick up* our order!

Like my dad always said, "Never trust a door-to-door salesman."

✧ ✧ ✧

What did the teddy bear say when someone offered him a cookie?

"No, thanks. I'm stuffed!"

✧ ✧ ✧

Devon has worked hard at rehabbing from her TBI by exercising and eating healthier.

Still, one thing you will never hear around our house is, "All right, who ate my kale?"

Devon makes for me what she calls "zero-labor tacos". Really, it's merely just eating my taco over another tortilla. And when stuff falls out—boom—another taco!

"The forecast calls for intermittent showers of lettuce, tomatoes, cheese, and beef."

What is an elephant's favorite sport?

Squash.

I'm not so sure we'll go back to a new restaurant we recently tried. When I asked the server how they prepare their chicken, he told me, "Nothing special. We just tell the chickens they're going to be the main course"

Our pizza delivery guy is so stupid. I, The Amazing Jeffo, paid him with quarters I kept plucking from behind his ears.

I read that ginger settles the stomach. So, I tried 20 ginger cookies for dessert. Anybody got a Tums?

✧ ✧ ✧

My three favorite things are eating my family and not using commas.

✧ ✧ ✧

Last week, Devon was hit hard with a virus. After many days, she groaned, "As long as I'm sick and stuck here on the couch unable to do anything, at least I'd better be losing weight!"

Poor thing, she's sicker than I thought!

✧ ✧ ✧

Did you know that when a clock is hungry, it goes back four seconds?

✧ ✧ ✧

I burned 1,800 calories yesterday. I really need a new oven timer.

I am very particular about nutrition and what I put into my mouth. I am into eating clean. I always tuck two napkins under my chin.

"Are the bananas ready to eat?" I asked.

Quick with the comeback, Devon quipped, "I don't ripely know."

✧ ✧ ✧

Never wanting to be annoying, I prefer the passive-aggressive approach. Impatiently waiting for my dinner, I commented to Devon, "It's amazing how fast you can make the meal you suggested this morning."

"Are you trying to say you're hungry?"

"I suppose."

✧ ✧ ✧

"Hey Devon, what's that good smell?"

"I'm roasting a squash, but I forgot what kind. It's really big!"

Unable to resist, I said, "Big? Well, then it must be a *Sasquash*."

George W. Bush must have despised scotch liquor. I remember him saying, "Evil Dewar's".

Did you hear about the pessimist who hates German sausage?

He always fears the *wurst*.

✧ ✧ ✧

Checking first with Devon, I asked, "I'm gonna assume you aren't supposed to use a wooden utensil on Teflon because this pan says "non*stick.*" Is that right?"

✧ ✧ ✧

I went to the store to get a 6-pack of Sprite, but when I got home, I realized I had picked 7-Up.

✧ ✧ ✧

Two cheese trucks ran into each other.

De brie was everywhere!

✧ ✧ ✧

What do you get when you cross a vampire with a chef?

Count Spatula.

✧ ✧ ✧

I have Spam all over my t-shirt! Of course, it was *my* decision in the first place to buy it at the Spam Museum gift shop.

An effective way to lose weight is to eat in your underwear.

Restaurants will typically throw you out before you can overeat.

I really, really like Devon's chili. Last night I suggested we share some with my visiting buddy. This morning Devon commented, "Scott must have really liked my chili. He had two bowls."

Trying to hide my concern, I responded, "Is there enough chili left for tonight?"

After checking in the refrigerator, Devon said, "Well... there's enough for two small servings or one really big serving."

After several seconds I asked, "So...what are you having tonight?"

What is a breakfast meal that wards off evil?

An egg omulet.

✧ ✧ ✧

As much as I like it, given the choice of hearing a good joke or eating a spicy bowl of chili, I would choose a *gut buster* over a *butt guster*.

Devon burnt our Hawaiian pizza today.

I think she should have cooked it on *aloha* temperature.

Why did the jalapeño put on a tiny jacket?

He was a little chili.

While dining at an Asian restaurant, I overheard festive conversation coming from a multi-generational family. Devon described excited faces as the server placed Peking duck at their table.

At that point, I overheard a grandfather announce proudly, "Just leave the bill with me. I'll take care of it. Nothing I like better than the bill," he said, as he took the head of the duck and began nibbling around its bill.

Sadly, my obese parrot has died from overeating, but it's a huge weight off my shoulders.

The United States may have been the first to split the uranium atom. But did you know Dairy Queen was the first to split the banana!?

What do you call someone who cannot stick to a diet?

A desserter.

What do you get when you combine Asian food with Classical music?

Johann Sebastian Bach Choy.

✧ ✧ ✧

"YUCK!"

"What's wrong honey?"

"Lacey licked my spaghetti plate I set down."

"No biggie. We'll just put it in the dishwasher."

"But I've been eating my salad with the same fork that was on that plate!"

"You could use my bottle of sanitizer. It may not taste that good, but it's awfully effective."

Ruefully Devon responded, "I guess I'll wipe it off with my napkin and hope the vinegar kills the germs."

"Don't be too hard on Lacey. I'm sure her eyes are filled with regret and sadness about her faux pas."

"It's hard to tell. She's licking her butt right now. Where's that sanitizer?"

We love all the new third-party shopping services. Instead of going out and risking Covid, we conveniently have it delivered.

Shouldn't the Burger King live in a White Castle?

✧ ✧ ✧

On Devon's birthday, I made her a surprise meal. Unfortunately, our local fire department ruined my surprise.

"My own southern creation! Blackened Spaghetti!"

♦ Chapter 5 ♦

Holiday Hoopla

"I bought my brother some gift-wrap for Christmas. I took it to the gift wrap department and told them to wrap it, but in a different print so he would know when to stop unwrapping."
—Steven Wright, comedian[4]

On Mother's Day, Devon commented, "It's pretty sad when our dog is a mother, and I'm not."

I jumped in, "Honey, in no way does Lacey have a leg up on you."

Ignoring my incidental pun, she responded, "How so?"

"Both of you are mothers to dogs."

✧ ✧ ✧

An election volunteer read the ballot to me to officially register my vote.

On one hand, voting makes me feel responsible.

But how responsible is it to vote blindly?

✧ ✧ ✧

Why don't you hear knock-knock jokes on the 4th of July?

Because freedom rings!

✧ ✧ ✧

I was just struck with a booming revelation. Anyone ever remember 4th of July fireworks being canceled because of rain? No wonder why our forefathers scheduled the thing on the $4^{th.}$

✧ ✧ ✧

"Why do I have such a hankering for pie?"

"Because you're so pastriotic."

Our neighbors, who were apparently confused about the date that commemorates Independence Day, were still blasting fireworks on October 19th this year and, in the process, were greatly upsetting our dog.

As the noise continued, Devon grabbed her bag of tension-relieving essentials and pulled out a Bully stick and Lacey's Thundershirt, which is a snug-fitting wrap that somehow comforts a stressed-out pooch.

I can appreciate such alternative methods of stress relief.
Occasionally I sniff a little bottle of lavender oil myself, which is kept handy on my side table. Lacey must have noticed. *En route* to finally settle in her favorite resting spot, she paused at the side table and deliberately sniffed my lavender bottle for several moments. "If it keeps Dad calm and better able to toss me treats, it's gotta be good stuff!"

For the record, a person born in 33 was 45 in 78.

A wonderful family gives me a ride to church on Sundays. Last week everyone in the car erupted in singing me the Happy Birthday song. I proceeded to excitedly share what Devon had gifted me:

"She downloaded high-definition recordings of Beethoven's *Overtures*, Schubert's *String Quartets*, Bach's *Suites for Cello* and Tchaikovsky's *Swan Lake*, not to mention the soundtrack from the Ken Burns *Country Music* documentary!"

Before I could add any additional details, an alarmed voice exploded from the far back of the vehicle. Addie, a concerned 6-year-old, cried out, "But didn't she get you any presents!?"

✧ ✧ ✧

I heard Ole and Sven are producing a sci-fi horror movie about an extraterrestrial creature terrorizing an Antarctica station.

It's going to be called *The Ding Dang Ting*.

Devon said to me, "Jeff, you can't start your trick or treating till it's dark."

"Until it's *dark*? I better get going! I'm already 45 years late!!"

Did you hear about the bedbug wedding?

They are getting married in the spring.

✧ ✧ ✧

My birthday is October 30th. This year, I tried a new tactic—extend any favors and privileges that might arise out of the goodwill of celebrating this wonderful time of year.

"Afterall Devon, it's only been X number of days since my most special day..."

Devon responded, "To be fair, I'll let you do that until the midway point between your birthday and mine on November 18th."

Mulling it over for a second, I said, "Well, I guess that's fair."

Devon quickly added, "And then, after my birthday, we'll do the same for me. I get favors and privileges until the midway point between my birthday and yours."

We enjoy watching scary movies around Halloween. After viewing *The Mummy*, I am struck how I missed out on a great opportunity. Those burial wrappings would mask my deficient acting skills and highlight my qualities. Facial expressions and voice training wouldn't be necessary. Thanks to my rheumatoid arthritis, moaning comes as second nature. Moreover, bent fingers and a stiff leg that I essentially drag slow me way down.

Self-promoter? I should be ashamed!

"I wonder if Boris Karloff started this way?"

"How 'bout for your special birthday dinner, I make your favorite meal, top sirloin?"

"With all my favorite sides? Sure," I eagerly replied.

But as the day went along, Devon's taxing online duties and house cleaning exhausted her resources. Sadly, she inquired,
"Do you mind if I just order in a nice dinner for us instead?"

It took our meal over two and a half hours to arrive, and it was missing my fruit salad. Devon bemoaned, "I'm so sorry. I'd rather wish these problems on myself."

As we began to wolf down our overdue dinner, we heard desperate knocks coming from the door to the downstairs living area.

"Devon, can you lend us one of Jeff's canes? Mike sprained his ankle," cried Mollie, my sister-in-law.

The amygdala (the injured area of Devon's brain) responded reflexively. Given that it's the center for fight or flight, she jumped off the couch—practically running—as she grabbed a cane in the process. Fortunately, I wasn't using it at the time.

When Devon returned to the couch, her amygdala fired once again as she caught Lacey, gulping the last portion of her dinner—sides and all.

To summarize, Devon went from having sympathy with my little plight, to empathy, merely in one hard swallow.

Chuck
RIB
Short Loin
Round
Brisket
Plate
Flank
Shank
LACEY!!

How do you manage a pumpkin addiction?

With a pumpkin patch.

What do you get if you divide the circumference of a pumpkin by its diameter?

Pumpkin Pi.

On Sunday, Devon turned 55 years old.

I said to her, "To symbolize the distinctiveness of your 55th, I have a surprise gift for you—double nickels."

"Double nickels?!"

"Yeah, I don't want anyone saying about my wife, 'She doesn't have *two nickels* to rub together.'"

For Devon's birthday, I thought it would suit the occasion to order in breakfast. What's more, Lacey did not object.

We finished our meals and shared the crumbs with her. Much like the operation of a skilled crime scene investigator, Lacey scoured every micro-section of our containers and wrapped up the case by licking each one of Devon's fingers. I can only imagine Lacey (while so precisely sniffing each delicious digit) thinking, "If there were only more clues, I know I could solve this caper! ...Hmmm...capers! Yum!"

I remember the time I handed my dad his 70th birthday card. He looked at me with tears in his eyes and said, "*One* would have been enough."

If my mom had her way, she would eat only beef. She has never liked chicken, fish, lamb, pork, and especially turkey. So, you can imagine her surprise when we seven children invited ourselves over to have a turkey-based Thanksgiving dinner with her in her assisted living dining room.

"I hope you all enjoy yourselves. I'm not coming," she threatened.

Eventually, she became resigned to the horrible idea of the family having Thanksgiving dinner together. After I became weary repeating again and again that a total of seven people would be at the table, I said to Mom, "It might help you remember if you can think of us as the Seven Dwarfs. I'll be Happy, and we'll have Bashful, Doc, Sleepy..."

She interrupted, "You can call me Grumpy! Besides, Devon isn't going to be part of that nonsense!"

"I'll just command her to do it," I responded.

"If you ever commanded *me* to do anything, I'd tell *you* where to go. You see, your dad and I had minds of our own."

"It might have been less explosive between Dad and you if you hadn't been so concerned about expressing your own minds, but if you had been a little more aware of the fallout that comes from explosive minds!"

ZZZ
ZZZ
CLINK
ACHOO!!

For Christmas this year, I gave Devon brand new beads from my old abacus. After all, it's the little things that count!

Devon's Korean language group is having a Christmas party and will exchange white elephant gifts. This time I definitely want to avoid what happened years ago when Devon and I attended a similar event.

Though it was advertised as a white elephant party, the generally upper-class attendees were exchanging things such as cut-glass candlestick holders, soap gift baskets, and even a 10" TV. We brought a figurine of a Martian holding a talking Magic 8 Ball that gives vague predictions of your future.

I remember at the time Devon whispered to me, "I hope nobody saw me add it to the gift pile."

This time, however, in all sincerity and good intention, I said to Devon, "At your Korean party, we have to give something of value. Since we have been cleaning out my magician closet, how 'bout we put together a collection of novelties and practical joke gags? But just the good stuff: Blow up Legs, Exploding Chocolates, Nose Flute, Rubber Chicken Keychain, Potato Gun, and...a recording of *The Original Vintage*, 'International Wind-Breaking Contest'. I'm sure some of that will get a lot of use."

Less than enthusiastically, Devon responded, "Yeah, we'll put a label on the gift that says: 'Almost Amaze and Slightly Delight Your Friends'."

Once again, it's Christmas—the time of year we express love for one another by wrapping something special. Of course, everyone enjoys the childlike wonder of trying to guess what may be inside the colorfully adorned packages.

Well, a wrapped package doesn't fool me! What does, however, is that after opening the thing I'm still wondering what it is.

To get around these challenges, Devon and I have come up with our own little solutions.

At the exact moment I pull away the last of the wrapping paper, Devon, in her best subliminal voice, quickly murmurs what the gift is. Then, *chop-chop*, I exclaim astonishment and simply repeat out loud what I just heard!

What is Scrooge's favorite instrument?

A tu-ba humbug.

Trying to be a thoughtful husband, I thought it would be nice to add a little stocking stuffer to Devon's presents.

Luckily, she had mentioned she likes Kohl's, so I jumped right on it and filled her stocking to the brim.

Why does Santa prefer to go down a chimney instead of a door?

It soots him better.

As we watched *A Charlie Brown Christmas* for the umpteenth time, I turned to Devon and said in my most sympathy-seeking way, "Did you know, honey, the very first time I watched this I was lying in a hospital bed?"

"How could I not know? Your reminding me of that has become as much of a tradition as the show!"

To express our appreciation for a family that drives me to church, we searched online for children's Christmas gifts. As we decided on several toys for their one to ten-year-olds, I noticed Devon's excitement.

I commented, "It's kind of fun shopping for kids, isn't it?"

In all innocence, she remarked, "Yeah. It reminds me of picking out something for you."

"Come on! I gave up Nerf guns at least three years ago!"

✧ ✧ ✧

After settling into bed last evening, Devon suddenly jumped up and headed to the living room.

"What's wrong, honey?"

"I forgot to turn off the outdoor Christmas lights along the wheelchair ramp."

"That's alright, no big deal."

"No! I have to turn them off, or Santa's GPS might mistake them for runway lights!"

• Chapter 6 •

A Light Bulb Goes On

"I think something is missing in my life...like...2-3 million dollars."
—Mark I. Roesler (friend)

Episode from the Get-a-Lifetime Channel's *Documentary of an Oblivious Wife:*

"Well, I can't say there was anything that exactly stood out, but in my gut, something felt a bit off in our relationship. I don't know...maybe three to four years into our marriage, one day I looked into Jeff's eyes, and there was nothing. The sudden realization shook me to the core.

"For a long, long time I wanted to rationalize that he simply, like many men, wasn't totally in touch with his feelings and evidently couldn't face that level of intimacy that can only be most deeply expressed between a couple through direct eye contact. Instead, I settled for cheap substitutes. More often than not, he'd peer into my nose, stare intimately at my eyebrows, or gape at my ear, but rarely into my eyes, almost as if his actions were random!

"Sure, it's easy to say now: 'Devon, how did you miss what was so obvious?' Now it's all as clear as day, but then...I was so blind to the truth!

"Admittedly, he wasn't exactly what you'd call a perfect driver, but in retrospect, the pieces now paint a much clearer picture: driving over four lanes of freeway traffic, through golf courses and big-box stores, under bridges absent of roadways...

"I'm almost beginning to think there might be a connection between my PTSD issues today and Jeff's stubbornness and unwillingness to be forthright about his situation. Throughout these years I unfairly blamed myself for what many unsupportive types (so called friends) kept saying, *that I wasn't paying close enough attention as a passenger*.

"But thank God, today I can look in the mirror and with conviction say, 'Devon, those horrible experiences that you suffered through for far too many years were not your fault, and you will no longer accept that they were merely *shortcuts* as Jeff would so glibly explain!'

"A tremendous weight came off my shoulders when I finally admitted to myself, 'This man has more than lazy driving habits going on here!'

"Eventually, with much therapy and self-examination, I came to what can only be described as a personal epiphany: 'Gosh dang! I think this man is blind!'"

Brought to you by *JeffreyAlity.*

✧ ✧ ✧

A commercial promoting a lady's razor came to our attention. "To guarantee a smooth shave, it comes equipped with an irritation defense bar."

Excitedly Devon jumped in, "I could use something like that around here with *you*!"

✧ ✧ ✧

Whenever you go to the bathroom, I hope it reminds you of one of my books. Do not get me wrong. Consider my latest book as a "bathroom reader". The added bonus is, if you're caught short of toilet paper you will have my book handy! That means regularly replacing your copy. A win-win for everyone!

✧ ✧ ✧

Did you know that 97% of the population is stupid?

I'm glad I'm in the other 5%.

✧ ✧ ✧

I tell my friends that *I* run things at my house: the vacuum cleaner, the garbage disposal, the washing machine...

In an otherwise uneventful day, I shared my latest news with Mom, "Devon just got me new socks that prevent itching!"

She replied, "Are your legs itchy?"

"Yes. Devon needs to lotion them."

"Don't wait for Devon. Why don't you just lotion them up yourself?"

Having just talked to Mom about my rheumatoid arthritis, I simply answered, "Because I'm stiff as a board!"

"You seem flexible enough when you want something."

"Well, on this one, I'm just not going to bend."

There is a new graphic software on the market. But it really sucks. It is called Photoshop-Vac.

Every day I play the Alexa version of *Jeopardy*, and afterward, she tallies my score. In her most minimal/positive way, she will report, "Congratulations! You've scored in the top 100% of players."

It's encouraging to know that I'm just as smart as the dumbest darn person on the face of the earth!

Students no longer bring an Apple to their teacher.

Teachers today are very much PC.

What is the difference between a step stool and a 3D printer?

The former is a ladder, and the latter is a former.

A telemarketer interrupted a phone conversation I was having with a friend. Unknowingly, I answered. He was selling replacement windows.

"I'm not interested. Our home is only about 15 years old."

The disruption to my call was bad enough, but he was loaded and ready. Changing his selling tactic, he resorted to a vaudevillian approach.

"Are your windows all functioning well?"

I replied, "They're hanging in there."

He quickly interjected, "Or would it be more correctly said, the windows are *double*-hanging in there?!"

✧ ✧ ✧

My fourth book is going to be a real page turner...175 blank pages.

One of the benefits of being blind occurred to me when I was in school: teachers never saw me continually feeling my Braille watch under my desk!

✧ ✧ ✧

Are you tired? There's a nap for that.

✧ ✧ ✧

"I just learned from a podcast that back in the 1940's General Motors surged ahead of Ford Motors. Their approach was to offer a variety of automobile brands, based on their level of quality, in all colors."

Half listening, Devon responded, "I can still remember my hard-working dad getting his first Oldsmobile."

Curious, I asked, "What kind of Oldsmobile did your dad like?"

Devon quickly responded, "Used."

Why is the letter B so cool?

Because it's sitting in the middle of the AC!

Perhaps it's a sign I don't get out enough, but...we have a caller I.D. that pronounces the name on the display and the phone number of the caller in an artificial voice. It interprets any combination of letters to be a word even when it's an acronym. Being it's an election season, we try ignoring the calls when we realize it's one of those never-ending political appeals. But, the acronym of one of the two major political parties, when pronounced, sounds like someone is stifling a sneeze, so I amuse myself and say, "God bless you!"

Does everybody do this kind of thing, or is it just me?

✧ ✧ ✧

When someone calls you a "nobody", just remember: nobody is perfect.

✧ ✧ ✧

I read in the Bible that the reason I sin is because of the fall. It's too bad we can't just go right from summer into winter.

I match my socks all by myself, by thickness, but I usually ask Devon to put them on me. After grabbing a fresh pair, she exclaimed, "Honey, these socks don't match."

My bubble being burst, after having folded all the laundry, I lamented, "Oh no! Next you're going to tell me there's *another* pair in the drawer that doesn't match!"

Anyone can be a winner...unless, of course, there's a second contestant.

✧ ✧ ✧

If you're not a fan of MLB, said abbreviation holds no meaning, and you should skip the following anecdote:

Nelson Cruz, the finest Twin's hitter in years, strongly recommends to teammates, a daily nap.

Results following the first round of play-off games indicate Nelson should have specified—not during the game!

✧ ✧ ✧

Is it true that plumbers prefer their wives to wear plunging necklines?

✧ ✧ ✧

Why does it cost so much to buy these shoes for my blocky feet? Their explanation: they charge by the square foot.

"Great! They fit perfect!"

Advice:

Do not think you are going to end up with a bottle of fine wine by leaving out a previously opened bottle of grape Gatorade for six weeks.

Learn...from...me.

✧ ✧ ✧

How disappointing it truly is when someone offers you a Junior Mint when you imagine they mean some sort of smaller version of the Federal Mint.

✧ ✧ ✧

I figure my best shot at becoming a scratch golfer is to wear sandpaper underpants.

✧ ✧ ✧

Musing one evening, Devon said, "Before I met you, I felt like Cinderella."

"How do you mean?"

"Growing up, I had very little, so moving into your new house was like being in Disneyland."

Surprised to hear this, I responded, "But we're not rich."

"I never had a dryer, dishwasher, water softener, ceiling fans, central vac, garage..."

Before leaving the room, she added, "Oh, another thing...a husband."

✧ ✧ ✧

War is not about who is right. It is about who is left.

I do not know anyone who carries himself better than me, which is kind of ironic as I sit here in my recliner.

These days you hear about virtual doctor appointments, virtual dating, and virtual church.

Well that's nothing. As an ostomate, I've been *virtually* going to the bathroom for years!"

I just read that 4,415,323,785 people got married last year.

Not to be picky, but shouldn't that be an even number?

✧ ✧ ✧

I read that babies who eat a lot of carrots, end up with orange-colored tips on their noses. I'm guessing, therefore, Cheetos must be full of the same kind of nutrition, because my fingertips also turn orange.

✧ ✧ ✧

Based on the sheer amount of Lacey's fur I move around every time I vacuum, I might as well be taking her on a walk!

How come builders are afraid to have a 13th floor, but book publishers aren't afraid to have a Chapter 13?

I'm reading a horror book in Braille. Something bad is going to happen. I can feel it.

I lost my job at the bank on my very first day. A woman asked me to check her balance, so I pushed her over.

✧ ✧ ✧

Devon read on *Buzzfeed.com*, the real reason why Mayberry was so peaceful and quiet. Nobody was married. Here are the single people that come to mind: Andy, Aunt Bea, Barney, Floyd, Howard, Goober, Gomer, Sam, Ernest T. Bass, the Darling family, Helen, Thelma Lou, Clara...

In fact, the only one married was Otis—and he stayed drunk.

✧ ✧ ✧

Reiki is an alternative therapy to treat stress. The practitioner positions their hands over a patient and, *voila*, the stress disappears!

I read about a stressed-out wife who expected way too much out of this therapy. She hoped by holding her hands over her husband that *he* would disappear!

✧ ✧ ✧

Why couldn't Mozart find Beethoven? Because he was Haydn.

I think military standard operating procedure is a great method of organization, especially with names: last name first and first name last. I overheard a group of Air Force veterans say, "We're not Fonda, Jane."

✧ ✧ ✧

A commercial came on advertising the coming Osman Shrine Circus.

Playfully, I yelled, "The circus! Let's go to the circus!"

Devon calmly responded, "We can't. It's Lent."

"Lent?"

"Yeah. My parents told me you can't go to the circus during Lent."

After a long pause, Devon quietly added, "Wait a minute! Do you think they only told me that because they didn't want to go or couldn't afford it?"

"I don't know...you better pull out your old Catechism book and look up 'Circus'."

Devon whimpered, "It's the old Easter Bunny/Santa Clause trauma all over again."

Playing harmonica reminds me of America's National Defense...they both require having a strong air force.

What do responsible hillbilly athletes wear?

A hiccup.

Those Breathe Right strips look *so* stupid, so I just use a rubber clown nose to cover them up.

If a marionette were promiscuous, it would have no strings attached.

I'm an organic version of NVG (night vision goggles). I can see just as well at night as I do in the day!

Just curious...if a crack forms in your driveway, is it your fault?

Actors in slapstick movies apparently all have metal implants in their heads since everytime they hit them, you hear a metallic sound.

Never trust an atom. They make up everything!

I wrote a book, and no one is buying it!

It's a book that explains a method to teach yourself how to read.

♦ Chapter 7 ♦

On the Same Page of Different Books

"Your secrets are safe with me. I wasn't even listening."
—Anonymous

What I respond to Devon, when she is in another room: "I CAN'T HEAR YOU, THE LAUNDRY'S GOING!!"

What she hears: "Very interesting; tell me more!"

I respond: "HONEY?! WHAT DID YOU SAY?"

What she hears: "Let's see how long we can keep this conversation going."

To unwind, Devon often watches *Judge Judy*. Though Devon's nature is quiet, sweet, and kind, I suspect her interest in the program is that she can safely live vicariously through the stern, no nonsense judge. In the middle of one of these episodes, I excitedly came out of my office to announce what I considered good news, "Honey! Honey! Guess what!"

Instantly I was silenced by a loud "Shush."

Not offended, I apologized and changed to a whisper. I assumed from habit that Devon was reminding me her TBI symptoms cause her to be sensitive to loud noises. Devon started laughing and said, "That wasn't me! That was Judge Judy!"

Thanks to Judge Judy, I must gird myself against the ever-increasing likelihood of a wife who runs a tight ship and makes me toe the line—all to have order in the household!

Originally, I was not so sure my future wife was interested in me because she would say, "Come over, there's nobody home." I went over, and sure enough, nobody was home.

✧ ✧ ✧

I was on the phone with a friend discussing the possibility of getting a new mortgage that would have a lower monthly payment, but at a higher interest rate. My buddy was recommending that we stay with a lower interest rate that included a higher monthly payment.

Explaining my reasoning, I said, "We don't want to go that route. Devon doesn't need that ongoing stress in her life."

Catching only my last few words, Devon looked right at me and exclaimed, "Stress or not, I love you, honey! Of course, I want you in my life!"

I stayed up all night to see where the sun went.
It finally dawned on me.

To our dismay, Alexa is becoming a part of our family. Last night as I climbed into bed, I belched. This is exactly the kind of noise Alexa assumes to be a word and responds with something like, "What did you say?"

Now she is letting her maternal instinct be heard. Immediately following my belch, she uttered, "What do you say!?"

We were watching a movie late one evening, and Devon said, "I could really use a nice, hot cup of coffee." But just as quickly, she changed her tone, "No, I better not. When I drink coffee, I can't sleep."

I interjected, "Funny, in my case, it's the other way around. When I sleep, I can't drink coffee."

This morning Devon received an email from Amazon. She became immediately interested in what was written in the subject field: "A book you'll love!" About this time, Devon was looking to relax with a good book since she had just spent the last year dedicated to working on my autobiography. Both writing and editing had been the primary activity that had consumed her free time.

The e-mail read, "We have a recommendation for you."
Excitedly she read on. "Hello Devon Smith, based on your recent activity, we thought you might be interested in this:" Displayed was a picture of *my* book, *Seeing Light in the Darkness*, with a link to purchase it on Amazon.

"Recent activity?" Devon sighed. "They must mean the activities of breathing, eating, and sleeping this book!"

By the way, she has a copy.

✧ ✧ ✧

Yesterday I looked everywhere for my book on anger management...I just lost it.

✧ ✧ ✧

If you have read my autobiography, you know the book's cover has a picture of me driving a sports car.

Well, right before the photo was taken, I had just finished a call to Devon from my cell phone.

"Honey, how does my new cell phone sound?"

Devon responded, "If you insist on driving, please be careful! I heard on the news that there is a nut driving the wrong way on the highway!"

"*One* nut? There are *hundreds* of them!"

HONK!!
SCREECH
XKY-204
ONE WAY

Walking into the kitchen, I heard a lovely tune being sung, and I asked, "Who's that singer, Alexa? Oh yeah!" I suddenly realized, "It's got to be Diana Krall!"

Devon excitedly said, "Finally! You recognized her voice. I'm tired of identifying her for you all the time."
I explained, "The only way I was able to tell it was her was that I really didn't recognize her voice at all. So, I figured if I don't know who it is...it must be Diana Krall."

My wife said I worry too much. But who wouldn't be concerned enough to ask their insurance agent about the possibility of losing coverage if lightning bugs hit our house?

✧ ✧ ✧

I sat next to Devon to watch a movie and said, "Honey, please turn up the volume."

"But there's no talking going on right now."

Knowing it was a movie I really liked, I replied, "Please turn it up."

Frustrated, she responded, "But there's nothing being said!"

I argued, "But it's my favorite. I'd like to hear nothing better."

✧ ✧ ✧

I knew I had artistic ability early on when my mother would set me on the porch, and I would draw flies.

Before I met Devon, I was so dense to the ways of romance that I went to the library and checked out what I thought was a guidebook to love. Turns out "How" to "Hug" was one of the "H" volumes of the Encyclopedia.

I was going to tell you a joke about time travel, but you didn't like it.

While busy making coffee, Devon entered the kitchen and asked me irresistibly, "Can I have a hug when your hands are free?"

"Well, I can more naturally do it with two."

It occurred to me that a barking dog would not scare away a burglar who was deaf. I think a more effective defense is to have an ornamental tree. When he sees the bark, the same purpose will be served!

✧ ✧ ✧

With the office door open between Devon and me while I worked, Devon announced from the next room, "I'm going to be studying my Korean."

Trying to be a considerate husband, I asked, "Am I making too much noise?"

Devon responded, "Only when you talk."

If anyone is wondering whether using a support cane to put on a pair of sweats is a good idea, let me speak from personal experience...It's not! This morning, I accidentally put on my sweats with the pull cords in the back. They didn't feel right, but I wasn't going to go through the effort of redoing it. To avoid looking like a doofus, I just turned my sweatshirt around, with the image on the back, and walked backward the rest of the day!

I'm ALWAYS thinkin'.

I heard the diesel fuel industry is trying to move ahead of the gasoline industry. Part of their campaign includes their new slogan: "We're passing gas."

Honesty can actually be compatible with marketing. A line of luxury cars whose engines cough, were simply renamed: "Croup de Ville."

✧ ✧ ✧

I learned to play the mouth harp by taking the *One Step at a Time* harmonica course. The entire first year, I just held it out the car window.

✧ ✧ ✧

I have taken up speed reading. I can read *War and Peace* in 20 seconds. After that, I read the author's name.

My disabilities perfectly jibe with old fashioned superstitions about the wedding day—namely, before the nuptials, the groom does not see the bride.

Joining my honey in the living room, I asked, "What are you watching?"

Devon answered, "It's a Dr. Phil show about over-controlling husbands."

I blurted, "Turn that off right now! I command you!"

Reassuringly Devon said, "Don't worry. You may be a little manipulative, but you're not too controlling."

"Gee! I thought I was more controlling than manipulative. Now I'm all confused."

I wish Devon were a little clearer with her messages. A guy could easily misunderstand what she is trying to say.

Today she said, "Honey, would you step back a little. You know I have a nut allergy."

A medication that Devon takes is called Amantadine, to help her mental clarity following her brain injury. When I remind her to take it, I say it in the clearest, most precise manner possible.

I do not want to end up discovering one day she thought I had been saying, "Don't forget to take a man today."

✧ ✧ ✧

I once won first prize from a martial arts competition after walking into a spider web.

The last renter of our lower-level apartment needed to relocate for work. After moving, his mail continued arriving at our house. We put it in a large envelope and mailed it to his new address, knowing soon the change of address would become official with the post office.

Today we received a post card from the USPS Department of Address Change. It stated, "The change of address security division forwarding system confirms and validates your change of address."

Right message, wrong address. This bureaucratic blunder should not surprise me. Our former tenant had received a postcard with the same message that was intended for the *previous* occupant of his new apartment.

✧ ✧ ✧

Sitting next to Devon while she was focused on her iPad, and I on the Minnesota Twins game, excitedly I blurted out, "Wow! Miguel Sano just hit his 3rd home run of the game!"

Putting up with the distraction of my game despite a total disinterest in the sport, to clarify, Devon asked, "Did you say 30 home runs?"

"Wow. You're willing to believe he actually hit 30 home runs tonight just because you so love and trust whatever I say, no matter how ridiculous it sounds...Thank you!"

I am trying to find out what the lowest rank in the Army is, but every military office I call keeps telling me it's private.

Unfortunately, the only Pepsi left in the house was covered with dust. "Ugh! This Pepsi tastes terrible," I gasped.

Devon responded, "Maybe it's flat."

"I don't think so," I said, "But I can't understand. I even cleaned the top off with disinfectant!"

Rather than bothering to look up the phone number of Lacey's veterinarian, I relied on my memory. Instead, I ended up calling a private residence.

While Devon looked up the right number, she said, "All the numbers you dialed were right except the prefix was 451, not 450."

"Jeepers. I was only one digit off. You'd think that would count for something!"

✧ ✧ ✧

I want to train to become a professional hip-hop DJ, but I know absolutely nothing about it. I'm just going to have to start from scratch.

✧ ✧ ✧

Getting out of my recliner, making a big deal about very little, I announced, "I'm going to fold laundry now. Is it on the island ready for me? I don't want to waste time standing around."

"So that explains why you've been sitting so long, huh?"

✧ ✧ ✧

These days I do not need to use bar soap. I can get by with a can of blind cleaner.

Blind
Cleaner

You do not have to be a genius to come up with inventions. The strength of my latest creation is based on its simplistic operation. I named it the "EtchaPad". It's about the size of an iPad. You operate it with two simple knobs in the corners... And, best of all, if you make a mistake, all you must do is shake it. I'm waiting to hear approval from the Patent Office.

Recently they wrote: "We sure hope you're not in a big hurry."

I figure they must be backlogged.

I was thrilled when my dentist told me he was going to honor me with a plaque...or was he telling me I had plaque??

I heard something sounding like Devon's voice break through my daydream. Not being sure exactly what I had heard, I said, "I love you, too."

After a moment or two, I added, "Is that what you said first?"

Caught off guard, she responded, "Well... I thought it!"

Attempting to let her off the hook, I replied, "I love you too, I think."

✧ ✧ ✧

Someone stole my Microsoft Office, and they are going to pay!

You have my Word!

Starting to tell Devon about an old friend I had just run into, she interrupted, "Do you know if she has any kids?"

"Yes. She had a baby boy a couple years ago. But I don't know how old he is now."

"A couple years ago? Then he's got to be at least 8 by now."

I snapped, "Are you trying to make me feel stupid?"

Devon replied, "Not at all...I'm just letting you talk."

✧ ✧ ✧

"I don't have anyone to talk to," my mom lamented in our daily conversation from her apartment at assisted living.

I jumped in, "Well, haven't you been talking to me for the last 90 minutes?"

She countered, "Yes, but when you hang up, you'll at least have Devon to talk to."

Overhearing our conversation on speakerphone, Devon spoke up, "Martha, I ignore him most of the day."

Mom persisted, "I wish I had someone here to irritate me."

"I'll send Jeff right over."

✧ ✧ ✧

Devon says to me, "Are you listening!?"

I thought, what a weird way for her to start a conversation!

Countless times Devon has reminded me to change the toilet paper roll so as not to leave certain people stranded.

After a renewed effort, I proudly announced, "Have you noticed I've replaced the roll twice in a row?"

"Actually, I think you've done that before," she answered.

Ever-craving praise, I continued adding to my consecutive replacement run to make it impossible for her not to notice.

But, after hearing Devon respond in the same lukewarm manner each time I announced my latest achievement, I realized just how clever she truly is.

Realizing Devon had been working for hours in the office, I said, "You need a break. Why don't you come out and make me something to eat?"

✧ ✧ ✧

After hearing Jeff talking to someone on the phone in the other room, he came out and said, "I just have to say how much you're worth to me."

I thought, "How sweet of him." What I hadn't realized is that he had just finished a conversation with a life insurance agent.

✧ ✧ ✧

I'm a natural motivational speaker, helping people acquire an attitude of gratitude. All I need to do is sing a short song; when I stop, people are overwhelmed with gratitude!

Hallelujah!!

♦ Chapter 8 ♦

Paws for Effect

"I don't want to adult today; I just want to dog. I'll be lying down on the floor in the sun. You can pet me and bring me some snacks." –Lacey B. Smith

"You can trust your dog to guard your house, but never trust your dog to guard your sandwich." –Lani Lynn Vale[5]

Who says we're wrapped around Lacey's finger?!

She doesn't even have fingers.

I share with Devon the same sweet memories of being transfixed to Saturday morning cartoons...*Porky Pig, Bugs Bunny*, etc. This Saturday morning, Lacey happened to receive her monthly supply of treats from her BarkBox subscription. The doggy delectables vary in type month to month. Pork and rabbit nibbles were the flavor this month.

Devon waxed, "Our daughter carries on our same childhood love of Saturday morning cartoon characters. But in her case, rather than watching *Porky Pig* and *Bugs Bunny*, she eats them."

Even if her monthly nibbles are reruns, I don't think she'll ever lose her taste for cartoon characters.

Lacey is so independent.

When we give the command, "Lacey, come!" the look on her face says, "Okay...but it better be good."

Alright, we indulge our dog! We've equipped her with a doghouse to suit the most discriminating canine tastes. It is outfitted with climate control, piped in music, a comfy couch, and a fully stocked pantry for treats on demand. Lacey thinks of it as comfortable; some consider it unduly spacious. Truthfully, it's a bit over 1100 square feet. We're just grateful she allows us to live there with her.

✧ ✧ ✧

I'm so cheap, that before we adopted Lacey, I said, "Why buy a dog when I can bark myself?"

Lacey used to be owned by a locksmith. We know this because, as soon as we got her inside, she made a bolt for the door.

Did your pooch make it this year to the Doggy House of Horrors at the Minnesota State Fair? I heard it is unbelievably scary. It is rife with every imaginable monster including blender, ear drops, vacuum, bathtub, running garden hose, fireworks, smoke alarm...and yes, even the dreaded nail clipper!

Devon asked me if I thought Lacey was spoiled.

I said, "No, I think all dogs smell like that."

Devon has commandeered my comfy kitchen stool.
She says, "I love this chair; it's just so comfortable." But I don't believe this is the real reason.

Typically, Lacey pesters Devon when they are on the couch together. Being aware of this, I responded, "The real reason you like my chair is that you can sit far away from the maddening crowd, i.e., Lacey."

Emphasizing no disloyalty to her four-legged baby, she explained, "Well, it's like when you put a toddler into a highchair to give the mom a break. Only, I'm in the highchair taking a break from my baby."

With all the news you hear about "bitcoin," who would have thought that our late dog, Krypto, could have come up with the concept of *crypto* currency...being the lousy speller he was!

Thank goodness Lacey never pursued politics! She has a definite character flaw—susceptibility to being bribed. When a service technician enters our home, Lacey assumes an intimidating stance and off-putting stare, sometimes accompanied by a perceptible rumble from her throat.

But, if the individual offers a little treat, Lacey immediately grabs it, becomes relaxed and, I am quite positive, in so many words, says, "I'm sure we can come to an understanding...Aw heck, let's cut to the chase...Is this your absolute best offer?"

After Devon had an enjoyable play session with our pooch, she said, "All in all, I'd definitely have to say I'm a dog person."

"Okay, then fetch me a snack."

With the coronavirus slowing everything and everybody down, Lacey has been spending lots of time on the couch.

I commented to Devon, "Hmm...'The Girl On The Couch'... kind of sounds like a famous painting."

Devon retorted, "Definitely a *still life*!"

Lacey is not only our beloved pet, but has proven herself as a socially conscious canine. As the biggest shedder in our household, she operates a community outreach to winged families in our backyard. Every day our girl delivers nesting material to nature's homeless.

I returned home concurrent with the highlight of Lacey's day—mealtime. After inhaling her dinner, which always leaves her with that wonderful feeling in her tummy, it was her mission to share her joy. She zoomed around to find me, did a happy dance, and snorted repeatedly as a safety valve to keep from exploding. Contentedly, she settled on the couch having shared the "good news."

Boy, if I believed what *she* preaches, I'd be fat and unsaved!

What Lacey lacks in pure intellect she makes up for with street smarts. Instinctively she knows I've got a soft heart and I'm an easy mark for a fast treat. Devon chuckles whenever Lacey sees me eating something.

Lacey's standard M.O. is to first stare at me for a while. She eventually realizes a staring contest with a blind guy never works.

Then, she turns her attention to Devon and gives her best smile and cutest pose as if somehow that should charm Devon into making me share my food. Lacey knows on some level that food opportunities somehow come through me.

But what else would you expect from an expert who plays both ends against the middle?

"Dad, did I ever tell you how much I love you?"

In a quiet moment on the couch, Devon said, "It's really sweet what you told me about how Lacey lies in front of the window alongside the front door waiting for my return."

Starting to doze off, I said, "She can do it for hours."

Further descending into half-slumber, I rambled on... "Sometimes when you're gone, I like to lay by the window aside Lacey...then sun myself on the back deck...and perhaps lay under the maple tree, waiting for a squirrel...or cool off on wet leaves under the lilac bush. And..."

Breaking my reverie, Devon exclaimed, "Wait! What?!"

Snapping out of my dream state, I responded, "Oh dear! I think for a few seconds Lacey was channeling through me!"

✧ ✧ ✧

To be able to concentrate on conversations more easily with foreign language partners, Devon closes the door in the adjoining room. Every time she does this, Lacey, Devon's little shadow, panics and runs after her Mama and starts scratching the door, which makes me cringe.

Last night, I yelled, "Devon! Open the door before she ruins it!"

Devon opened it and responded, "Well, it's just like the old axiom: 'Spare the door; spoil the dog'."

✧ ✧ ✧

When Devon asks me, "What would you like me to make for dinner?" I respond, "You might as well ask for Lacey's input. Like Lacey always says: 'Two meals, three mouths.'"

✧ ✧ ✧

The other night we heard a sort of barking sound coming from outside our front door.

"Woof-da, woof-da."

Confused, Devon opened the door.

No wonder!

It was a Norwegian Elkhound. So, I threw it some Lefse and the barking stopped. That should be the last we hear from him!

Lacey is so jealous of Devon's attention that whenever my kind wife puts on my socks, Lacey sticks her muzzle right in the middle of the process, regardless of consequences. Today Devon was using a sanding block to remove a callus from my foot. Lacey ended up looking like she could model for a doggy dandruff commercial!

I'm grateful Devon doesn't hold grudges. She thinks, contrary to what my mom feels, that our Lacey looks simply adorable. Whereas, when the aforementioned furry namesake was brought up at our weekly game of Gin, mom commented, "I tell you, she is one ugly bugger! When God was making her, midway through He changed His mind twice."

There are two reasons we put in a doggy door for Lacey.

#1.

#2.

✧ ✧ ✧

Devon takes a medication to increase cognitive clarity because of her TBI. I am no doctor, but I think it might be time to "up" her dose.

After again having to wipe Lacey's fur off my pants, I said to Devon, "Lacey is such a shedder we really should have called her cheese."

Confused, Devon responded, "Cheese?"

Explaining, "Haven't you ever heard of Shedder cheese?"

Groaning, Devon answered, "Please tell me it's time to take my Amantadine."

Blind jokes are okay if they're funny. Take it from a resident expert.

Two guys were walking their dogs. One had a German shepherd, and the other, a chihuahua. The owner of the shepherd suggested going into a bar for a drink.

The other man said, "They're not going to let dogs into the bar."

The first guy says, "No, watch this!"

So, he puts on some dark glasses, acts like the German shepherd is a seeing eye dog and walks into the bar.

He orders a drink, and no one says anything.

So, the second guy takes out some dark glasses, flips them on, and walks his chihuahua into the bar.

The bartender says, "Sorry, we don't allow dogs in here."

And the man says, "It's okay; it's my seeing eye dog."

The bartender laughs and says, "This chihuahua is your seeing eye dog?"

And the guy says, "They gave me a chihuahua?!"

Do NOT
Pet

Following an extremely tiring day, the next morning Devon could not stop yawning.

"Your yawning is so exaggerated, you sound like you're acting out a story to children."

Being the ham I am, it spurred my own storytelling scenario. As I began imagining out loud, my voice became sing-songy: "The Untold Tale of a Golden Rescue Dog and its New Parents."

Devon interrupted my regaling. "Oh, Lacey has sat up, her ears are erect, and she's very interested in what you're saying."

I could tell Lacey was crawling up to me to apparently have a better seat for the rest of the story. Charmed by her sudden interest in what I was saying, I continued:

"The poor scared rescue dog had no mom or dad. One day she was adopted by a nice couple named Jeff and Devon. As her parents showed love and patience to the scared little newcomer, she gradually became comfortable in her new surroundings and totally took over the joint and, for all intents and purposes, became the head of the house. Over time, she knew in her heart that her loving mom and dad were easy marks, but patiently worked with them until they became putty in her paws and personal attendants to all her whims.

"The End."

Our stubby-legged, barrel-chested dog has a definite "alpha" personality. Devon and I, who very much love one another even with ongoing challenges, must stay together—you know...*for the sake of the pack*.

This morning, I gave in and shared the leftovers of my high-quality *Evol* brand meal with our pooch. The microwavable product is expensive, but I feel it's a good value since the food is hormone-free, non-GMO, and highly nutritious. Besides, if I'm gonna spoil Lacey, I like the idea of sharing what I think is *real* quality.

As I heard Lacey licking up every essence of its nutritious goodness, I commented, "Wow! Our doggy really has discriminating taste."

As a loud cracking noise commenced, Devon added, "I agree. She's even choosy about what kind of plastic tray she eats!"

✧ ✧ ✧

Without Major League Baseball around during the pandemic, I made do by having Lacey catch Milk-Bones I threw her way.

"Stop! I'm walking by," Devon warned.

With a Milk-Bone in hand, I responded, "I don't think you have to worry about *this* hurting you."

"No, but I'm worried I may hurt *you*."

✧ ✧ ✧

We signed Lacey up for an auto-ship program to receive a doggy treat and toy each month. At least the $20 per month supplies us with high quality products.

"Devon, listen to Lacey. She is playing that squeaker toy like a Stradivarius! It's got to be putting out a 3-octave range!"

In a pleading voice, Devon asks, "Is blood coming out of my ears yet?"

"My next song, and a personal favorite, 'Puppy Love.'"

♦ Chapter 9 ♦

Romance Alley: Gutter Balls & All

"You don't have to be crazy to hang out with me...I'll train you."
—Anonymous

Advice to husbands: Before you tell your wife something important, gently take both her hands into yours.

That way, she can't hit you.

Devon read a story to me about a Chinese farmer, who painstakingly took sixteen years to teach himself law so he could stop a chemical company from polluting his town. It took so long, because he traded bags of corn for permission to read law books over thousands of nights at a bookstore. Devon exclaimed, "Sixteen years? I can't even imagine! That's how long our entire married life has been."

"It would seem more like forty years to me."

Who says being married does not have inherent danger?

After all, there is an IED in the word.

✧ ✧ ✧

After dinner, I asked Devon for a cookie. Upset, she responded, "Will you please give me a break! You've been asking me to get you all kinds of things tonight."

"Like what?"

"Well, you want me to vote for your favorite Minnesota Twin for the All-Star game, take your blood pressure, find something to watch from the DVR, and now a cookie!"

"Gee, I'm getting the sense that maybe something is bothering you."

I never got my cookie.

✧ ✧ ✧

Seeing me struggle with an unwieldy task, Devon sympathetically said, "That would bug me too—but you still bug me more."

Once Devon and I saw a marriage counselor. I agreed to join her there directly following one of my magic performances.

She opened the session and said to the counselor, "He has ceased to amaze me."

Devon said to me, "You should be happy you're not a Greek tragic hero type."

I responded, "Thanks. It's nice to get a little respect around here."

Devon cheerfully explained, "Tragic heroes have but a single flaw. You have lots of 'em!"

"Devon, I think it's so cute how you unintentionally interchange Lacey's and my name when she's being naughty. Just like a grandmother would confuse names."

"Did you also notice, dear, that it happens only when I'm annoyed?"

I once gave Devon the silent treatment. At the end of it, she said, "For the first one or two minutes, I thought I was just imagining it. Then, after five minutes, I thought it was some weird joke of yours. But now that it's been an entire ten minutes, it's become obvious! You broke your gabber!"

"A marriage should be based on honesty, right Devon?"

"That's right!"

"Good, because I'm feeling really lazy this week. So, would you mind doing my dishwashing duties?"

Devon answered, "I'm sorry. It just wouldn't be right."

I replied, "Well, maybe not, but do the best you can."

Devon told me that I twist everything she says to my advantage. I took it as a compliment!

When Devon gets a little upset, sometimes a simple, "Calm down," in a soothing voice, is all it takes to get her a lot upset.

Devon got mad when I told her I absolutely must hang out with my buddies on Friday nights, and, that it's *non-negotiable*. She hates my mandates!

I shared with Devon that Johann Sebastian Bach once walked 230 miles to hear a concert. She quipped, "I'll bet he still made his wife get up to change the TV channel."

✧ ✧ ✧

Outvoted 1 to 1 by my wife. Again...

✧ ✧ ✧

In a reflective moment, after a particularly challenging day, Devon said, "I love you. I don't know how you put up with me."

"Oh, pish-posh. I don't know how YOU put up with ME!"

Though spoken in a comforting tone, she said, "Everybody else has to."

"Hmm."

✧ ✧ ✧

Devon had just sat down again after her umpteenth trip getting me items from the kitchen.

I said, "Could you also get me a napkin?"

Frustrated, she grumbled, "I need to stand up for my rights!"

In a quieter voice, I said, "You are absolutely right, honey! But as long as you're standing up, could you get me..."

✧ ✧ ✧

"Please, go potty! All your wiggling around is making me nervous!"

I responded, "Your nervousness is a result of our spiritual bond that comes from being married."

"What are you talking about?"

"Well, the Bible says, 'The two of them become one'[6] ...couldn't that also apply to '*Number 1*'?'"

This morning Devon asked, "Do you know what day it is today?"

She sure can scare me easily!

Curious about a lyric, Devon asked Alexa, "Play 'Iron Man', by Black Sabbath."

I immediately responded, "Oh, no. That song is evil!"

Devon retorted, "Well, you listen to 'Frankenstein' by The Edgar Winter Group, and *that's* not Satanic?"

"But honey, 'Frankenstein' doesn't even have words!"

Defending herself, Devon said, "Well, deaf people can go to hell too!"

✧ ✧ ✧

We listen to podcasts of old-time radio shows in bed at night before getting sleepy. Last night the announcer introduced the radio drama by saying, "A Story of a Man Who Lived as Long as He Kept Talking".

Devon murmured, "This is all too familiar."

"You've heard this story before?" I asked.

Devon sighed, "Heard it? I've lived it!"

✧ ✧ ✧

I love being married. It's so great to find that one special person you want to annoy for the rest of your life.

By the way, the best way to always remember your wife's birthday is to forget it one time.

✧ ✧ ✧

Never get involved with a tennis player because love means nothing to them.

Devon heard a loud crash from the bathroom where I was readying myself. She leaped off the couch, fearing I had fallen, and strained her neck in the process. Later, the pain in her neck reminded her of the relief she had received from a chiropractor following her auto accident.

Though she rarely prioritizes her needs, Devon announced, "I'm going to make an appointment with a chiropractor. There's no good reason I should deny myself."

I added, "You're absolutely right, honey. That's my job!"

Devon tells me I am always under foot.

I keep telling her that's because I'm her sole mate.

For starters, perhaps watching *Judge Judy* and ordering groceries at the same time may not be the best idea. As Judge Judy yelled at her litigants, Devon unloaded her just-delivered groceries. Regretfully, she discovered she had not ordered her favorite brand of hair product.

Later, still upset and steaming about her mistake, she commented, "I'm glad Judge Judy gets crabby at her litigants. Then I don't feel like I'm the only one."

Trying to be an encouraging partner, I said, "You're not crabby. Being crabby is a *public* display."

In a voice only I could hear, I added, "But that's all I'm gonna say...and *keep* it public."

✧ ✧ ✧

After overhearing Devon in the kitchen cry out in frustration about spilling her coffee, I offered an unwelcome suggestion, "Maybe you should hold items with both hands."

Later I dropped my phone in the bedroom where I could not reach it and asked Devon for her assistance.

From the kitchen, I heard, "Well, maybe you should hold items with both hands, dear."

In my best Dickensian pronouncement, I responded, "She uses my own words against me."

Her quick reply, "I may seem quiet, but I'm busy keeping score until the time is just right!"

✧ ✧ ✧

The latest headline reports that wives are treating their lazy husbands with the medication, Pitocin, to make them begin labor.

✧ ✧ ✧

Give a husband a fish, and he has food for a day; teach him to fish, and you can get rid of him for the entire weekend.

✧ ✧ ✧

Husbands should listen more to their wives.

My ears perked up, and my pride soared when I heard Devon compare me to Plato.

But the part I did not hear: "*Pinching your butt*...I think of Play-Doh."

✧ ✧ ✧

You do not have to marry for money; hang around the rich and marry for love.

Devon was riveted by today's *Dr. Phil* theme of people who have been scammed by their significant other.

Angered, Devon said, "Those scammers are evil. And these stories break my heart."

"Have they ever had any *blind* gimpers on there that have been scammed by a disloyal partner?"

"No...You'd be the only one."

I asked Devon, "How would you describe our love life?"

She quickly responded, "Our love life is like a fairy tale...Grimm."

✧ ✧ ✧

We are grateful for a grant program because Devon receives a modest stipend to be my PCA (Personal Care Attendant). This, however, does not give me an excuse to not participate in household chores to the best of my ability.

One duty of mine is folding laundry. I've already exhausted the expected fallback excuses, such as, "*Out of sight, out of mind.*"

So today, Devon gently reminded me, "There's a basket of unfolded towels and underwear with your name all over it."

I responded, "I was hoping that would have come out in the wash!"

✧ ✧ ✧

What a day!

After preparing for a custom magic show, searching in vain for supplies, and wrestling with a funky computer, I groaned loudly to Devon, "Can you bring me a big glass of wine? I'm just not used to all this stress...other than the kind *I* cause."

Finishing breakfast, I flipped off my custom bib that looks like a magician's vest.

"Hey! You're flicking your dirty napkins on the floor! And where are you going?" a puzzled Devon asked.

"Isn't it obvious? I can't stand the heat, so I'm getting outta the kitchen."

✧ ✧ ✧

I asked Devon what she wanted for Christmas.

She replied, "Nothing would make me happier than a diamond necklace."

So, I bought her nothing.

I started walking again on the treadmill, thinking maybe it would get Devon's competitive juices flowing. I look for different opportunities to draw my wife into my competitiveness, but she rarely bites. Pointing out to me that competitiveness shouldn't always be my aim, she said, "You're so competitive! If I jumped out of an airplane and both my parachute cords failed, I can see you jumping out and yelling, 'Oh! So, you wanna race, huh?'"

✧ ✧ ✧

Devon was excited as she eagerly opened the mail to read what she assumed to be her first Merry Birthday greeting...or so she thought.

When my Devon, my beloved, the one who perfectly fills my heart, my very queen, looked at the envelope, she read, "*The words you wish you said to Angela years ago—even more precious and meaningful to her right now. RSVP, while you still can, Jeffrey.*"

If thinking that opening the envelope might have provided a chance for me to be exonerated, forget that!

What Devon read inside did its very best to seal my fate:

"*Dear Jeffrey, please don't let another day go by without telling Angela how much she means to you—always has and always will. Just imagine the look on Angela's face when she reads these magical words: 'Angela, I loved you then, I love you still, I always have, I always will. Jeffrey.'*"

It continued, "*With diamonds, jeweled hearts, and the words you'd wish you'd told her so many times...EVERYTHING about this gift says, 'I love you, Angela'.*"

I'm gonna guess that this little mailer has resulted in more accusations and fights than sales! If you're gonna get one of the names wrong, let it be mine and at least give Devon a cheap thrill.

A long time ago I knew that sales were in my future.
I am so good I could sell a watch in heaven.

Devon and I had an argument as to which is the most important letter in the alphabet. I won.

✧ ✧ ✧

My wife treats me like God. She ignores my existence and only talks to me when she needs something.

✧ ✧ ✧

Musing one day, I asked, "Have you ever thought of us taking dance lessons?"

"I think it's hopeless. When you dance, it looks like you're getting the Heimlich maneuver from the Invisible Man."

✧ ✧ ✧

I felt so flattered because the other day someone said to me that I looked like The Hulk.

"Is that because of all my muscles?"

"No. It's because you have grass stains all over your clothes!"

✧ ✧ ✧

As I came out of the bathroom, having just showered, Devon excitedly exclaimed, "Do you realize there's a moon on both sides of our house?"

Incredulously I blurted, "How can that be?"

She responded, "I just realized it after you walked by me on your way out of the bathroom."

✧ ✧ ✧

My ex-girlfriend still misses me. I am kind of worried...her aim is steadily improving!

✧ ✧ ✧

Devon asked, "Why do you so often wear wet socks in the winter? "The very thought of changing them gives me cold feet!"

I have trouble reading Chinese fiction. Too many characters to keep track of.

I can't tell you how much Devon does for me! Her kindness is only surpassed by her capability.

"Honey, when you're done making lunch, I'd like us to contact the post office for rates to mail my books."

Devon justifiably responded, "Jeffrey, you need a Man Friday. No...you need a Man Saturday, Sunday, Monday, Tuesday, Wednesday, and Thursday!"

♦ Chapter 10 ♦

Show-It-Off Biz

"Sometimes showing off produces results." —Natalya Neidhart[7]

"I am a great admirer of mystery and magic. Look at this life - all mystery and magic." —Harry Houdini[8]

I did a magic show yesterday wearing my new suspenders. The show went off without a hitch!

Before beginning a show, I ask, "By a round of applause, how many of you have seen me before?" If there is no applause, I say, "Don't feel bad. *I* haven't even seen *me* before."

I was getting ready for a Cub Scout show the other night when I said to Devon, "Cubbies have to be my favorite audience."

Devon replied, "It's no wonder...You're right up there with their maturity level."

After giving it considerable thought, I nodded and said, "Yeah. I think you're right."

✧ ✧ ✧

During one of my tricks, I hold up a length of rope that is tied in the middle. I ask the audience, "Name the city in North Dakota, where I got this rope...Minot."

"You're the greatest audience I've never seen!"

✧ ✧ ✧

Returning home from a magic show where I did not use my microphone/amplifier, I commented to Devon, "Do you realize that when I talk really loudly, I never stutter?" Devon, who relishes a quiet home, sighed, "You certainly don't stutter around here."

If you believe in telekinesis, raise my hand.

This is the time in my show when I normally saw a woman in half. Unfortunately, the woman I normally saw in half is no longer around.

No, it's not what you all think. She's happily married and lives in Duluth...and Cleveland.

✧ ✧ ✧

For those of you who say life is an illusion, "Life" is a trick I'm working on for my next show.

✧ ✧ ✧

As Devon was helping me get into my magic show duds, I said, "Every performer should have his own professional dresser."

Devon responded, "I'll be your professional dresser if you'll be my Sugar Daddy."

"I would gladly go to that expense, except you have diabetes."

Without missing a beat, Devon retorted, "Okay. Well, then you can be my Stevia Daddy."

Always wanting to have the last word, I responded, "That sounds Splenda!"

✧ ✧ ✧

Devon is considering a new career in magic. She already has decided on her stage name: *Miss Direction*.

Hear about the Mexican magician who said he would disappear in front of everyone?

He said, "Uno, dos ..." and then he disappeared without a trace.

"Move along, folks. Nothing to see here."

If a magic volunteer seems nervous when I pull out my hand chopper trick, I reassure them, "Don't worry, I have the name of a good secondhand shop."

✧ ✧ ✧

Some Cub Scouts can be filled with ideas lots bigger than themselves. I mentioned after my show that I had some small inexpensive magic tricks for sale. A little scout came up and said, "I really like your first trick, the vanishing bottle."

I replied, "That's one of my favorites too."

After several seconds of silence, I sensed he was becoming annoyed.

Unable to contain his frustration, he sputtered, "Well, then, how much does your magic stand cost?"

✧ ✧ ✧

I've been accused of making a chain of islands vanish.

Come on!

It was just an Aleutian.

✧ ✧ ✧

Before an audience, I sometimes display a red *letter P*, and say, "I'm kind of concerned. My urologist is worried about the color of my pee."

✧ ✧ ✧

"For those of you in the back, who can't see, join the club!"

I made a bold business move. But, if you do not take risks, you'll never get ahead. I heard the cost of buying airtime for a 30-second ad on this year's Super Bowl is $5.6 million.

I said to myself, "Amazing Jeffo, go for it!"

I know it's expensive publicity, but I figured the additional magic shows I'll get from the fantastic exposure will cover my cost. Let's see...based on my standard fee of $350 per show, I'll only have to do 16,000 shows to break even. After that, the rest is gravy!

Hmm...I better start eating *way* healthier.

As a part-time magician, I can honestly tell people, "Now you see me; now you don't."

Just to keep up with the competition, Devon accompanied me to watch a stage magician and his wife assistant.

We were not impressed when he performed his "sawing a woman in half trick". We happened to know that the magician had a wife with no legs.

✧ ✧ ✧

The new game show for paranoiacs is called: *The Price is Right Behind You!*

We watched a magician who made bottles of wine instantly appear.

He calls himself the "Grape Houdini".

The Tonight Show, starring Johnny Carson, became such a bedtime ritual that many people thought Johnny's ears were actually in the shape of big toes.

After a trick, I tell a volunteer that he did a good job and deserves a little freebie.

So, I hand him a miniature *letter B*.

✧ ✧ ✧

Listening to the news, we heard that the Department of Education was cutting off funding for the Special Olympics.

Wistfully, I commented to Devon, "I remember doing a magic show at one of their pre-Olympic trials."

Devon asked, "Were you doing the tricks as they sprinted by you? That sounds hard. 'For my next trick'...*Swish*... 'Well, I'll catch you on the next lap. Now you see it'...*Swish*... 'Dang, it! Somebody tell me when they're back again... now you don't!'"

✧ ✧ ✧

As a comedian-magician, I have made it my policy to present family-friendly entertainment, indoor or outdoor. But working in the frigid, finger-numbing cold of Minnesota makes it exceedingly difficult not to perform blue.

Amazing Jeffo is so funny that they have parades for him! Audiences march right out the door.

"A volunteer, please, for my flaming guillotine trick."

♦ Chapter 11♦

Take Two Laughs & Call Me in the Morning

"Never go to a doctor whose office plants have died."
—Erma Bombeck[9]

Scientists have invented a pill that prevents dehydration. You take it twice a day with a glass of water. It's probably all hype; otherwise, everybody would be doing it.

Does a hip replacement surgeon imply that the main hip doc is on vacation? Does it really matter after all? He's still hip!

My rheumatoid arthritis started in my hands years ago and ended with my fingers looking like a Picasso painting. On the bright side, I did actually inspire a popular 1970's, rock group—Bad Finger.

✧ ✧ ✧

It's no wonder Devon is so PC. She just cannot get away from it! She is my PCA and has PCS.

✧ ✧ ✧

Acupuncture is a jab well done!

✧ ✧ ✧

While waiting in my doctor's office, Devon commented that the bright lights were exacerbating her TBI symptoms.

She said, "I'm putting on my sunglasses, but I feel ridiculous doing that."

I responded, "It will make you look like Jackie-O."

Unenthusiastically she answered, "I feel more like Jackie-Oh *Brother*!"

✧ ✧ ✧

When I broke my leg in 2012, I decided to audition for a stage play. I wanted to be in a cast.

Nine out of ten mountain rams recommend Excedrin for fast, headache relief.

Devon and I were testing a new product for those like myself who have an ileostomy pouch. It was a skin prep wipe that creates a sticky surface for better pouch adherence. Devon noticed that everything touching the stickiness became equally sticky. "Why can't they make a sticky skin wipe that's not so sticky?! Is that so much to ask by a lady so hard to please?"

Why do nurses use red crayons?

To draw blood.

An inhaler made to calm coughing comes automatically with an added benefit—in middle-aged women, and up, it also prevents incontinence.

A type-A personality walks into a bar and orders everyone a round.

A blind man walks into a bar...and a table and a chair.

✧ ✧ ✧

Who says tag is only for young people? Just ask your dermatologist.

After Devon asked why I had not yet finished my dishwasher chores, I answered, "Honey, I think I'm just incapable of doing all the things you want me to around the house! Maybe I've got some kind of syndrome!"

Devon responded, "I'll tell you what it's called in plain English—you're lazy!"

Thinking more about it, I said, "Hmm, tell me the medical term for that so I can talk to my doctor about it."

✧ ✧ ✧

The latest medical release reports that the Grinch died yesterday of dilated cardiomyopathy.

I guess his heart really did grow three sizes!

✧ ✧ ✧

Upon entering the bathroom, Devon did not notice I had moved to the toilet to staunch a bloody nose. As I waited, I thought I might as well use the toilet at the same time.

When Devon looked over, she saw blood in the bowl. "Oh my gosh! You have blood in your urine!"

I responded, "Actually, I have urine in my blood."

After calming down, she said, "The first is not good, but the second could kill ya."

✧ ✧ ✧

I wrote a book about reverse psychology. Please do not buy it.

✧ ✧ ✧

Growing old is like living with inclement weather. You are never sure if the rumble is from distant thunder or your stomach, or, whether the feeling of sprinkles is from dark clouds or incontinence.

If a proctologist practices out of his home, would he risk arrest for running a crack house?

Devon and I both seem to have injured our right shoulders. The only decent joint between the two of us is where we live.

✧ ✧ ✧

After removing my basal cell cancer at the dermatologist, the doctor began cauterizing the wound, which created a weird, cooked odor.

I commented, "Smells like we could use a little barbecue sauce."

Devon jumped in, "Smells like ham to me."

✧ ✧ ✧

England has no kidney bank, but it does have a Liverpool.

✧ ✧ ✧

How do military personnel handle pain?

They go on Aleve.

✧ ✧ ✧

At the dermatology appointment desk, the receptionist looked at her schedule and said, "How does 10:45 A.M. on April 15th sound to you?"

I responded, "If it's going to be April 15th, shouldn't the time be 10:40?"

✧ ✧ ✧

They have new technology for the Wisconsin beer enthusiast who has sleep apnea. It's called the CPAP Blue Ribbon machine.

Why are pediatricians always in such a rush?

They have little patients.

(Sorry, that was kind of childish.)

I get bloody noses. Using a frozen gel pack typically staunches the drips. After walking around for a half hour with the pack strapped to my forehead, Devon asked, "How do you feel?"

"Well, to be perfectly frank, now I've got a severe head cold."

✧ ✧ ✧

Just because you are a left-hand amputee does not necessarily give you the right...

✧ ✧ ✧

Welcome to middle age, where no one ever told you rigor mortis sets in *before* you die.

✧ ✧ ✧

*Eureka (*or so I thought)! Upon hearing a commercial for Gold Bond for Dark Spots, I figured to be the perfect candidate.

Being blind, I have more dark spots than I know what to do with!

Back in 2012, my doctor told me I broke my leg in two places. I told him, "Well, I'm going to quit going to those places."

I told Devon last night I need to call the doctor to make an appointment.

"Which doctor?" she asked me.

"No." I said, "The regular kind."

If I, who am way beyond being merely legally blind, were to form an investigative news show, I would call it something like *400/400*.

Why did I fall down the well?

I could not see that well.

✧ ✧ ✧

Thanks to rheumatoid arthritis, I never had to show my ID to enter a nightclub. They just assumed I was plenty old given my cane and the way I walked.

✧ ✧ ✧

They do not tell you how dangerous stargazing is. I once did it all afternoon, and now I am blind!

✧ ✧ ✧

Would a podiatric intern be called a tenderfoot?

With the left speaker of my stereo suddenly not working, I am calling a doctor to report an acute case of mono.

When you are only sort of annoyed with having a cold, you are Sudafed up.

Turns out both Devon and I should have put on our Christmas wish list, a gyroscope. This morning as I hugged Devon, I apparently was more focused on the hug than the balance. "Oh! I'm falling backward!"

Adjusting, I responded, "I gotcha!"

She retorted, "Now I'm falling forward!"

"I gotcha!"

Still a little panicked, she said, "Just be *middle*!"

Two years ago, my doctor told me I was going deaf, but I have not heard from him since.

I like to hit people on the knee to test their reflexes. I don't know why. I just get a kick out of it.

✧ ✧ ✧

During an attack of laryngitis, Devon lost her voice completely for two days. To help her communicate with me, I developed an easy system based on taps.

"One tap will mean *give me a kiss*. Two taps will mean *no*. Three taps will mean *yes*. And 395 taps will mean that I need to do the dishes."

What do you say to a hitchhiker with one leg?

"Hop in."

✧ ✧ ✧

The inventor of the throat lozenge died. They announced at his funeral that there will be no coffin.

What did one DNA say to the other?

Do these genes make my butt look fat?

✧ ✧ ✧

I just read a list of *100 Things To Do Before You Die*. I was a little surprised that one of them was not "yell for help!"

✧ ✧ ✧

Someone from church volunteered to drive Devon and me to visit her brother, who was ill and in a transitional care unit.

Having never been to this facility, we stopped at the front desk and Devon asked, "Do we need to check in?"

The woman looked at us, briefly looked in her book, and responded, "Was he out?"

Confused, Devon responded, "I'm sorry?"

The receptionist pointed to me and repeated, "Was he out?"

"Oh, this is my husband! He doesn't live here. We're visiting my brother."

Impersonating a female voice, I blurted out what she might have been thinking, "Shhhure you're visiting. Grab him, Delores!"

Later I imagined her sheepishly saying to coworkers, "He sure looked like he belonged here."

"My name is Jeffery Smith! I'm married, and I live in St. Paul, Minnesota!"

♦ Chapter 12 ♦

That's What Friends Are For

"We will be friends forever because you already know too much."
—Anonymous

A local farmer had 96 cows on his farm. But when he rounded them up, he had 100.

My buddy's wife is notorious for always being late. When her daughter, who is normally on time, came late to church for the second half, her mother said to me, "Where is that daughter of mine? She's late!"

I said, "Isn't that the pot calling the kettle black?"

"No! Not at all!"

"How so?"

"She's never late. I'm never on time."

"Hmm. I see."

Why does Waldo wear a striped shirt?

He does not want to be spotted.

After several hands of Texas Hold 'em, my friend, Craig, flaunted his substantial winnings by shaking his bin full of quarters at the group. Rightly irritated, I blurted, "You're no dancer. Quit shaking your booty!"

✧ ✧ ✧

Devon was once engaged to a boyfriend with a wooden leg, but she broke it off.

If we ever need a defense lawyer, we have a friend who thinks outside the box. Currently, she only represents penguins. She explained that she wants to assure a judge that her clients are not a flight risk.

✧ ✧ ✧

Before leaving the car, having arrived at church, I asked my buddy Mark, "Can you tug up the tongue on my left shoe? It's scrunched up."

He said, "Let me go around to your side of the car."

"Can't you just bend over and do it from the driver seat?"

He responded, "My timber has lost its limber."

✧ ✧ ✧

I was ruminating about some of my wife's friends going through menopause. Without a doubt, they are some of the warmest people you will ever meet!

✧ ✧ ✧

When my friend Tom and I go out socially, I usually end up making him wait. But today, I was actually waiting outside for him.

As I boasted about my timeliness, he pointed out, "You still weren't on time. I was late because I had to wait for the garbage truck to leave your driveway."

I joked, "The garbage hauler asked me if I needed a lift."

He responded, "Makes sense! To them, you're just white trash."

After returning from bird hunting, Craig's son, Noah, joined our Texas Hold 'em game. He commented, "I hate holding still in the woods waiting for grouse when the mosquitos are ravenous."

I responded, "That sounds like the complaint of a military sniper."

"I'm no sniper!!"

Examining my cards, I replied, "The grouse may beg to differ."

A friend and I visited a local coffee shop. I can hardly believe the price of a cup of coffee these days! I ordered the Café au *Layaway*.

Recently, I visited a friend who was in Critical Care at the hospital. He happens to be from another country. I do not speak his language, but our friendship seems to transcend mere words.

Sadly, while visiting at his bedside, he expired. Because of the depth of our unusual friendship, his last words I shall never forget.

Immediately upon arriving home, I Googled their meaning:

"You're standing on my oxygen tube!"

✧ ✧ ✧

I have a friend who thinks drinking responsibly means not spilling it.

We were talking about me going to my buddy's cabin for the weekend. Devon said, "I'm glad you can go on a fun trip, but I have to say I just don't sleep well when you're gone."

Pleased, I asked, "...because you miss my comforting presence?"

She responded, "Oh, uh...ABSOLUTELY...and the white noise from your CPAP machine doesn't hurt either."

A friend of mine said he got gas today for $1.39. Unfortunately, it was at Taco Bell. The same friend does everything possible to ignore my advice on healthy eating. He says, "Eat donuts! They're the original hole food."

Forty years ago, in college, my buddy Mark would regularly invite me next door to his dorm room. Time and again, I thought it was because of my stimulating conversation. Unabashedly, he explained, "I have insomnia. The droning quality of your voice, like white noise, knocks me right out."

Ironically, today as a UPS driver, Mark calls me late at night to help him stay awake. I wish he'd stop flip-flopping on me!

✧ ✧ ✧

A family, including its carload of kids, gives me a ride to church every week.

One of their little ones asked me, "What does the word inexplicable mean?"

I said, "It's hard to explain."

✧ ✧ ✧

My friend, Craig, a devout Christian, loves cribbage so much that for his wedding, he originally planned to have a cribbage-themed reception.

He dropped the idea thinking it might be seen as hypocritical to have a Christian wedding followed by a peggin' reception.

I refuse to be part of a carpool without a life preserver.

My former blind mobility instructor (me, not him) and I waited at the counter of a local café to be served our java.

When the barista finally arrived, I asked, "Where have you been?"

"On a coffee break, where else?"

I told my pal Mark a typically dumb joke of mine, which for whatever reason, caused him to laugh. This reminded me of the process by which communicable diseases spread.

So, I said to Mark, "I was the host of that diseased joke. When you pass it along to someone else, you'll be playing the role of host."

Thinking about what I had just said, I asked, "As a UPS driver, wouldn't you already be considered a carrier?"

Mark immediately responded, "A common carrier."

✧ ✧ ✧

Out of the blue, I got a call from a friend. But isn't that to be expected? He's a pilot.

My friend told me his yoga teacher was drunk this morning. It put him in a really awkward position.

After returning home from visiting with friends at our local coffee shop, Devon noticed Mark and I gabbing away. "You seem to be having a good time chatting."

I responded, "Oh yeah. We're like a couple of old ladies yakking."

Devon stated, "You mean a couple of gossips."

Indignant, I snapped back, "I don't gossip! I just listen."

Devon added, "I don't know which is the bigger fib in that sentence!"

I often talk to a buddy who, because of the nature of his job, can schmooze with me pretty much any time. Today he phoned and said, "Jeff! I didn't hear from you yesterday."

I replied, "To tell you the truth, you just didn't come to my mind. I liken it to what a famous philosopher once said."

He responded, "What was that?"

"I didn't think; therefore, you ain't."

♦ Chapter 13 ♦

The Wisest of Acres

"I've had an extremely busy day converting oxygen into carbon dioxide." –Anonymous

With no disrespect to God, I feel I have been responsible for fifty percent of my own salvation. God has provided the grace and mercy part. My half has been the sin.

I am really bummed. They denied my submission to copyright the name of my new cosmetic surgery franchise—*Crater Joe's*.

Have you ever heard a joke with no punch line?

I signed up with one of those high intensity training gyms. Boy, did I have the wrong idea! Turns out all the members are actually cross and are having a fit!

Our local S.W.A.T. team has its own reality TV show—*Big Flash-Bang Theory*.

What is the only thing that Flat Earthers fear?

Sphere itself!

How do Flat Earthers travel the world?

On a plane.

What did the President do when he noticed a fly in his office?

He called in the S.W.A.T. team.

✧ ✧ ✧

When two egotists compete, it is an I for an I.

✧ ✧ ✧

A Frenchman would not know any Beatles songs, but a Norwegian Wood.

✧ ✧ ✧

Some believe as I do, that love trumps all...others ask if Trump loves all.

✧ ✧ ✧

With money around here being a little tight, I called our credit card company to whom we have been loyal for at least a decade, to inquire if they could offer us a temporary lower interest rate.

After a litany of explanations and my call being transferred to myriad departments, they flatly denied our request, but I must admit, in the most extravagant manner of politeness.

"Is there anything else I can do for you today, sir?"

"Just give me a moment while I try to figure out exactly what you have done for me today."

✧ ✧ ✧

My brother Mike went bald years ago, but he still carries his lucky comb. He just cannot part with it.

Most blind people are not able to draw, but I can. Ask anyone who has heard me play harmonica.

Get it? Or did I blow it?

✧ ✧ ✧

Would a Catholic church amidst an earthquake be considered a "quivering Mass"?

✧ ✧ ✧

In my life, I have cut down 173 trees. I know because each time I keep a log.

✧ ✧ ✧

I can always tell when someone is lying. And if I feel carefully, I can usually tell if they are sitting or standing as well.

✧ ✧ ✧

What do you call a priest who becomes a lawyer?

A Father-in-law.

✧ ✧ ✧

Back in my sighted days, I heard you could look at an eclipse through a colander.

I tried, but it just strained my eyes.

✧ ✧ ✧

I'm like a ninja at the gym because you'll never see me there.

✧ ✧ ✧

If you've never tried archery with your eyes closed, let me tell you—you do not know what you're missing!

Archaeologists have recently uncovered evidence that indicates the majority of Pharaohs were part of a pyramid scheme.

Where do naughty rainbows go?

Prism.

If a tree falls in the forest and nobody hears it, my illegal logging business is a success!

As Devon began to serve me dinner, she said, "Here's your bread and water."

...what did I do wrong?

I will tell you why I do not choose to have my ashes scattered. I have spent well over half a century trying to get my life together. I do not want to have to go through that all over again.

Why couldn't the musician tell a fib?

His lyre was in the shop.

I was approached about presenting a sock-puppet show. Luckily, my perpetually cold feet gave me the perfect excuse not to.

✧ ✧ ✧

Police were summoned to a daycare center where a three-year-old was resisting a rest.

It's a fact that a deer can jump higher than a one-story house! This is due partly to the position and length of their powerful hind legs, and partly to the fact that houses cannot jump.

✧ ✧ ✧

Hear 'bout the dyslexic man who walked into a bra?

✧ ✧ ✧

Since I so like to be the center of attention, you'd think I'd be looking more forward to my funeral.

✧ ✧ ✧

Reading while sunbathing makes you well red.

✧ ✧ ✧

When it comes to sharing your faith, be bolder, not a boulder.

✧ ✧ ✧

I believe the finest shoes are made of smooth leather.

My opinion will never be suede.

Late in the day Devon announced, "It's too hot in here. I'm closing the front window blinds."

Confused, I ask, "But isn't the east side the cooler side this time of day?"

"It's not my job to disprove it; it's my job to support it."

✧ ✧ ✧

I was shorted on my chlorine shipment the other day.

That's what I call dirty pool!

✧ ✧ ✧

I do not know why my heating bill is so high. If anyone knows, come on over and explain it. My door is always open.

✧ ✧ ✧

Green is my favorite color.

I like it better than blue and yellow combined.

✧ ✧ ✧

I am the Editor-in-Chief of a publication for procrastinators: *The Dally Times*.

✧ ✧ ✧

If a law is created to punish anyone for poor grammar construction, it should be appropriately called a "sin-tax."

What is more, the guilty should go to a correctional facility and serve their "sentence".

✧ ✧ ✧

Police arrested scam artist, John Young, who tricked people into buying some sort of substance he named the "Elixir of Immortality". Upon questioning, they discovered Young has a criminal record, being arrested for the same felony in 2004, 1965, 1923, and 1866.

The cable guy asked me what time it was.

I said between 1 and 5 pm.

✧ ✧ ✧

I am exhausted. What a workout! I just spent the last two hours boxing. On top of that, I had to carry the flattened cartons to the recycle bin.

✧ ✧ ✧

What has eight legs, eight eyes, and eight hands?

Eight pirates.

✧ ✧ ✧

Why are there so many Smiths in the phone book?

They all have phones.

✧ ✧ ✧

When we were all patiently plodding our way through Coronavirus, they told us we only needed masks and gloves to go out to grocery stores. They lied. Everyone else was wearing clothes!

✧ ✧ ✧

How did Superman make millions?

Flipping houses!

SUPER SMITH

"I know you've always wanted a family crest, but don't you think you're carrying it a bit far?"

♦ Chapter 14 ♦

Up & Outward Bound

"Sometimes, just getting out of the house and doing something you haven't done in a long time (or never done!) can open up the doors to inspiration." –Ken Hill[10]

Devon continues to work with her language partners to learn the Korean language and to help them learn English.

Today she received a text asking, "Do you know the shows *Scoopy Doo* and the *Brad Bunch*?"

Another language partner we deal with daily is Alexa. I asked her to set a reminder for Devon: "Give Jeff his shot."

Later the original message was translated as, "Give Jeff a head shot."

Devon chirped loud enough for me to hear, "I agree! Jeff sometimes needs a good head shot."

✧ ✧ ✧

Dutifully, Devon continues learning Korean. It is not uncommon for her to approach me and practice a Korean phrase, but I really never know what she's saying.

Today, during one of these incidences, I suggested to her, "If it would be of help to you, can you teach me how to say in Korean: 'Can somebody help me get this bucket off my head?'" ...that way, no matter how poor my pronunciation is, I'll be covered.

Jeff: I know the capital of every state in the union!

Devon: Oh yeah? Then what is the capital of Wyoming?

Jeff: Uh...That would be "W!"

When Devon uses her language learning app, she always screens the person before replying to their initial greeting. On occasion, a member might even hit on her. For example, members have commented, "Hey, beautiful, will you be my wife?"

Devon will respond firmly, "I don't think we would be good language partners. Good luck on finding someone."

Curious, I asked, "Do the comments ever get even nastier?"

"YOU BET! Then I BLOCK them."

"Like WHAT?!"

She muttered, "Hey, Grandma!"

✧ ✧ ✧

You are not supposed to bring your own snacks into the movie theater, but as a magician, I always have a few Twix up my sleeve.

✧ ✧ ✧

Devon's language exchange app is open to all ages. One day she said to me, "I'm getting a notification again on the language app from the man who's wanted to talk with me. Do you mind?"

Devon added, "Don't worry, it's totally innocent. He's just a harmless little old man in his 60's."

I didn't answer right away, so she asked, "Why are you looking at me like that?"

I growled, "Why do you think? I'm 5′ 6″ and 62 years old!"

✧ ✧ ✧

As part of Devon's learning about all things Korean, she ferments vegetables. Releasing the gases, following fermentation, disperses quite the unpleasant odor.

Devon informs me that the upside is that the effects of fermentation fill the air with a rich probiotic atmosphere. "We're going to have the healthiest guts around!"

Excitedly I said, "And our house will smell like guts too!"

I called into the living room, "What are you giggling about out there?"

"I'm talking with one of my Korean language partners who is interested in learning English. He just told me that one of his foot fingers hurts."

I asked my North Korean friend how he likes living there.

He said, "I can't complain!"

Vietnam must not have any issues with data privacy. According to the TV game show, *Jeopardy*, forty percent of Vietnam's population has a surname of Nguyen. It reminds me of the old joke about the mother who continued having children despite her general dislike of little ones because she was trying to lose herself in the crowd.

Today we defied the laws of physics. Riding down in an overly warm elevator, we disproved that heat only rises.

Since Devon's accident, she and I rely even more on the aid of UPS and Metro Mobility, which is a transportation service for people unable to drive. With both of us officially classified as driving menaces on the road, UPS delivers assorted household items to us, and Metro Mobility transports us when we need to go out.

Naturally, with my advertising background, I thought I would use a little creativity to show these organizations my appreciation for their assistance. Slogans are, particularly, my specialty. But my carefully crafted offerings, pro bono may I add, have all been rejected! I figured Metro Mobility riders would appreciate the large territory the service covers. And I thought UPS customers would be impressed by the predictability of receiving their packages...but *nooooo*.

What is so wrong about the slogan, "*We're all over the road!*"?

And regarding UPS, what is wrong with, "*We're doing fine...not too far behind!*"?

On a daily basis, Devon gets a variety of calls from new English learners on her language exchange app. Tonight, as she emerged from the other room following a 20-minute conversation, she was all aglow.

"Well, well. My language partner from Korea told me I was intelligent and professional."

I replied, "That's wonderful! What else did you two talk about?"

"We worked on his refining the pronunciation of 'intelligent' and 'professional' for about 19 out of the 20 minutes. The other minute or so was a bad connection."

Getting my haircut today reminded me of my late barber, may he rest in peace...

Maybe giving military buzz cuts at the Grateful Dead concert was not such a great idea after all.

I do not mind being called a blind magician for its marketing purposes. Placing the word "blind" before the word "magician" highlights my unique selling proposition.

However, as someone with disabilities, I have always felt it important to use "people-first" language, such as saying, "a person who is blind", rather than saying, "a blind person."

Lately, I have been teaching magic to a couple of little boys who are Korean. Every time they see me, they always cry out in Korean, "*Maseul Ahjussi*!"

After many lessons with them, one day I asked their mom what is the meaning of that pleasant-sounding phrase?

With some hesitation, she replied, "Middle-aged magician."

"Please tell them it's *magician* first. And then, only if there's time, that other stuff."

What happens when the smog clears from Los Angeles?
UCLA!

My transportation service uses a digital reader to charge fares. The driver announced, "This trip is free. My digital reader doesn't work!"

I responded, "Works for me!"

My brother, the cop, told me there's a guy in town stealing the wheels off police cars. They are working tirelessly to catch him.

✧ ✧ ✧

"What are you doing, Devon?"

"I'm messaging a Korean college girl who's having lots of boy problems."

"How nice that she's coming to you for advice."

"Yes, but I don't care much for the fact that she refers to me as 'Grandma', even though it's a title of respect in their culture."

"How 'bout those two, cute little Korean boys I entertain with magic at your language club? Their sign of respect is to call me, 'Middle-aged Magician'."

Devon reassured me, "Just think of the esteem you'll feel in 10 years when they call you, 'Old-Fart Magician'."

Is Japan part of a chain of islands?

Not *atoll*.

We shouldn't have been surprised that our cab driver got hopelessly lost after we noticed his name card: **Willy Nilly**.

As Devon faces challenges with learning Korean, it reminds me of my own struggles with the mother tongue. I remember growing up hearing, "Jeffrey! Were you raised in a pig sty? Go clean your bedroom!"

✧ ✧ ✧

I was involved in a language immersion program. I nearly drowned.

Devon is so focused on learning Korean grammar; her example is starting to affect me too.

"For your next birthday, how would you like a camping house?" I asked.

Confused, she responded, "Camping house?"

I said, "I'm just trying to help you by using the correct future tents."

✧ ✧ ✧

I understand there used to be some really challenging types of jobs, such as the poor car-parking valet of *circa* 1910.

"I can fetch your vehicle now, sir."

"Thanks. It's the black Model T."

✧ ✧ ✧

These GPS's have become so intuitive! Metro Mobility was taking Devon and me to a store that sells carpet.

As we approached the store, the GPS announced, "Your destination will be in 150 square feet."

✧ ✧ ✧

I did not realize that the opening of the Lego store was going to be so popular. People were lining up for blocks.

My new carry-on case has a slip of paper inside boasting that its construction will survive an airline crash. So I guess if the plane starts to go down, I can just climb into the case. They could also market the added value of the case, by having it double as a memorial on your mantle containing your bits and pieces!

Devon talks to people on her language app through text and audio. This evening, someone introduced himself as Anthony. After a short while talking to him, Devon began wondering if he was truthfully representing himself, which is a mandatory requirement of her language app. He posed as a 54-year-old man fully fluent in French, but native to the United States.

Devon: "I see you've traveled a lot. Is that for work?"

Anthony: "Yes, like I do am a businessman am in charge of transporting metal barrel."

D: "Metal barrels? What are they for?"

A: "It used for making of foods, alcohol, they are used for many industrial activities."

D: "You know, I don't mean to be rude, but I don't think you're a native English speaker, as you said. What is your true native language? Just be yourself because native English speakers can tell very easily who is and who is not."

A: "How you mean about that, wah you saying?"

D: "This is a prime example. It is not correct at all and is not anything a native speaker would say. So please stop representing yourself as a native English speaker. It's wrong and deceptive and against the rules."

A: "You're sounding really funny, huh."

D: "Prove me wrong then."

And that was the last we heard of Anthony. Using the most intensive cross-examination tactics to break down the cover of the most duplicitous imposters—that's my little wifey! She learned it all through her 25 years of teaching pre-kindergarten and determining who started what first!

✧ ✧ ✧

A member of Devon's Korean language group dropped her off about midnight. They had attended an authentic Korean dinner party.

She described the evening to me, "I really enjoyed all the time around the table, just talking and laughing. But I have to admit my rear end is killing me."

Having an opinion on all subject matter known to man (whether I know about it or not), I suggested, "With you not being able to exercise since your recent concussion, your rear end can get sore as you become a little softer. You need to build muscle back there again."

Mulling it over, Devon responded, "Yeah, I better restart my walking program."

I pontificated, "The more you walk, the more you'll be able to sit!"

"!?"

✧ ✧ ✧

As we sat in a lobby awaiting our ride, I reached toward Devon because she had packed me a drink. After revealing my intent, she feigned sadness and said, "Oh, I thought you were reaching out for a hug."

In a voice tinged with realism and a bit of facetiousness, I quipped, "At our age, wouldn't you rather stay seated than get up and give me a hug anyway?"

She laughed, not even arguing the point.

Conclusion

Why do Devon and I laugh so often at life's mishaps, inconveniences, and hardships? Are we not taking these challenges seriously? Seeing the funny in life, in a way, puts a hedge around us and gives us a sense of empowerment over the unavoidable circumstances.

Humor may help us cope, but faith is what ultimately sustains us. Our disabilities have humbled us and made it clear that we cannot do it on our own. God has supplied us with all our core needs: love, significance, and security. We have received love from each other and from friends who have encouraged us when we needed it. We have been given significance by being able to help others through the experience of our circumstances. And we have been blessed with security, as God has fully supplied us with our physical and spiritual needs.

While things may change from what we perceive as good to bad, God has never changed and has always been our Rock. We recognize that, despite obstacles, God's blessings have far outweighed our struggles and have sustained us through them. He has taught us patience as He unfolds His plans through His perfect timing.

"'For I know the plans I have for you,' declares the Lord, 'plans to prosper you and not to harm you, plans to give you hope and a future'." ~Jeremiah 29:11 NIV

Of course, we can butt heads at times, but we deeply love and respect one another. The Bible describes the effects of adversity: *"As iron sharpens iron, so one person sharpens another."* ~Proverbs 27:17 NIV

I believe our situations have made Devon and I stronger as individuals and as a unit, and we are able to have a more tempered attitude about life's unpredictabilities. Where one of us lacks, the other always fills in.

We have experienced again and again how, through challenges, doors have been opened and opportunities have arisen from what began as difficulties.

Devon and I hope you have enjoyed walking with us through our foibles and victories. We hope you have laughed and, perhaps along the way, gained a bit more understanding to carry you through your own trials

Notes

1. John 16:20b-21 NIV.

2. Dunfey, J. (Producer), & Burns, K. (Director). (2019). The hillbilly shakespeare (1945-1953) (Episode 3) [Documentary miniseries]. In J. Dunfey, (Producer), *Country music: a film by ken burns*. Florentine Films; PBS.

3. LaRoche, L. [@LorettaLaRoche]. (2015, October 6). Stressed spelled Backwards is Desserts [Tweet]. Twitter http://fb.me/4uw7xo3C7

4. Fenster, B. (2005). Laugh off: the comedy showdown between real life and the pros. Andrews McMeel Publishing.

5. Vale, L. L., (2014). Another one bites the dust. Createspace Independent Publishing Platform.

6. Genesis 2:24 (NIrV).

7. Natalya Neidhart Quotes. (n.d.). BrainyQuote.com. Retrieved May 14, 2021, from BrainyQuote.com Web site: https://www.brainyquote.com/quotes/natalya_neidhart_1008366

8. Harry Houdini Quotes. (n.d.). BrainyQuote.com. Retrieved May 18, 2021, from BrainyQuote.com Web site: https://www.brainyquote.com/quotes/harry_houdini_672676
9. Erma Bombeck Quotes. (n.d.). BrainyQuote.com. Retrieved May 18, 2021, from BrainyQuote.com Web site: https://www.brainyquote.com/quotes/erma_bombeck_100082
10. Ken Hill Quotes. (n.d.). BrainyQuote.com. Retrieved May 18, 2021, from BrainyQuote.com Web site: https://www.brainyquote.com/quotes/ken_hill_274859

We would greatly appreciate if you would kindly post a review about this book on Amazon.

Please check out my websites:

Amazingjeffo.com

Jeff-speaks.com

Other Books by the Author:

Seeing Light in the Darkness: A Story of Surviving Affliction with Laughter and Grace.

An autobiography about America's only blind magician with multiple disabilities. Jeff Smith demonstrates through his tenacity and sense of humor that a myriad of physical roadblocks cannot stop him from thriving, not despite his challenges, but *because* of the challenges.

Follow how a child immersed in the depths of despair was lifted by family, friends, and faith, which helped transform his turmoil into triumph. Filled with short, easy to read chapters and engaging photos throughout, this is an insightful, tender, and hilarious read.

Splashes of Laughter in the Storm: Seeing the Funny in Life's Tumbles & Trials. Jeffrey Smith is America's only blind magician/public speaker with multiple life-long disabilities. His wife, Devon, prevails over the ongoing effects of a traumatic brain injury.

In the wake of ***Seeing Light in the Darkness***, Jeff's motivational and humorous autobiography, readers will again be thoroughly entertained by ***Splashes of Laughter in the Storm***.

Together, Jeff and Devon share a humor-filled approach to life's unwelcome events. Enjoy amusing anecdotes that reveal how attitude and belief are key to overcoming anything. "*Our purpose and hope for this book are to encourage others to embrace life to the fullest, not despite challenges, but because of them.*"

Chuckle with the Smiths who possess the ability to turn simple miscommunications and everyday predicaments into hilarious outcomes. You'll be refreshed and encouraged!

Made in the USA
Middletown, DE
03 January 2023

20178107R00115